Kath[...] with best
wishes for a blessed
Christmas

Emmanuel Lutheran
Sunday School

1927

Dr. Martin Luther

MARTIN LUTHER

THE LION-HEARTED
REFORMER

By
J. A. Morrison

GOSPEL TRUMPET COMPANY
Anderson, Indiana

Printed in U.S.A.

To
The Youth
Of
The Land

INTRODUCTION

Great heroes are never-failing examples that help spur us on to noble endeavor. While we do not want to follow men so blindly that we lose sight of the Christ of God, yet there is room for conforming to the injunction of the great apostle, who says, "Follow me as I follow Christ."

Luther followed Christ. He was not humanly perfect by any means—who of us are? But, he did the right as God gave him to see the right, and it mattered not whether it was prince or pauper who tried to divert him from his path of duty, for he kept right on. His own indomitable character is reflected in that hymn which is so aptly called Luther's hymn, A Mighty Fortress Is Our God.

This life is not meant to be a students' textbook. It is a life of Luther that young people will like to read during spare moments. We trust it will inspire our noble young people to follow Luther as he followed Christ. To this task it is committed.

THE PUBLISHERS.

CONTENTS

Chapter I
A POOR BOY

On Nov. 10, 1483, when Hans and Margaret Luther laid glad eyes upon the face of their new-born son, they little thought or even dreamed that they were looking into the face of one who would not only change the destinies of nations, but who would change the aspect of human history for all time to come. It is said that every child is an unlocked casket of possibilities. On this memorable date of Nov. 10, 1483, God presented these humble German peasant parents with a casket containing possibilities, the extent and value of which will not be known fully until all human achievements will be brought to account.

When a boy who has poverty for his companion is inclined to find fault with the company that he is forced to keep, he should comfort himself by reading about the boyhood days of Martin Luther—a son of poverty who by the strength of God and the grace of Christ stamped his name on every page of history written subsequently to his day. Martin Luther did not inherit from his parents luxuries that money can buy, but he did inherit those sterling qualities of character that came into such good play when he was brought face to face with those battles that proved him a great victor. He inherited sturdiness of character, strong will-power, stedfastness of purpose, honesty of heart, and a religious disposition. He who falls heir to such should consider himself blessed of God and happy.

The Luthers were Germans. They lived in the Thuringian Mountains. If you will look at a map of Germany you will find that these mountains are located near the central part of that country. Nestled among these steep and beautiful mountains is the little town of Eisleben. In it Martin Luther was born and here he died. The very next day after Martin was born he was taken to the church and there baptized, for his parents were very religious people and they had been taught by their church that it was their duty as parents to have their children baptized as soon as possible.

Martin Luther was still a small baby when his parents moved from Eisleben to Mansfeld, where his father found work in the mines. The struggle to provide a living here for their loved ones was hard for Martin's parents. When he grew to be a man he had this to say concerning those struggles, "My father was a poor miner and my mother carried the wood from the forests on her back; they both worked their flesh off their bones in order to bring up their children." And "bring" them up they did. Martin, his brother, and his three sisters were not permitted just to "grow up" and do as they pleased. The parents taught their children religion—those days it was quite generally believed that religion could be most efficiently taught with the rod. Those were the days before the great religious Reformation, in which Luther was to have so large a part, had swept over the world, and the then prevailing religion of Roman Catholicism was largely a religion of ignorance and fear rather than a religion of knowledge and love. Luther's parents were devout Catholics and their strenuous and even unmerciful discipline of their children they believed was the very best for the children's welfare. Because Martin stole a nut one time his mother whipped him until the blood flowed. His father punished him so severely at another time that Martin could stand it no longer and fled from home. But when Luther had grown to be a man he did not harbor any bitterness in his heart against his parents. He remembered their awful grind of self-sacrificing toil and knew that they had toiled because they loved him and his brother and sisters, and because they desired to give them proper food, clothing, and education. In speaking of the severe punishments which he received from the hands of his parents, he remarked, "They meant it well from the depths of their hearts, but they did not know how to distinguish the dispositions to which punishment is to be adapted." In later life when God had given him greater light on things religious and when through him this light had been shed over all Europe and even over all the world he saw that the severity of his parents had only reflected the dark, legalistic spirit that had pervaded their age.

As I have said, Luther was taught religion in his boyhood home at Mansfeld; but such a religion as it was! It was a religion without love, and such religion is always bondage most grievous. His mother gathered the children around her knees and told them of the Father and Christ. But what sort of ideas of God and Christ did Luther get in those hours of early piety? Hear what he says in later life about it: "From early childhood I was accustomed to turn pale and tremble whenever I heard the name of Christ mentioned, for I was taught to look upon him as a stern and wrathful judge. We were taught that we ourselves had to atone for our sins, and since we could not make sufficient amends or do acceptable works, our teachers directed us to the saints in heaven, and made us to call upon Mary the mother of Christ and implore her to avert from us Christ's wrath, and make him inclined to be merci-

ful to us." The Luthers, in accordance with the
times in which they lived, believed in all sorts of
supernatural influences. Luther says that in his
childhood he had a constant dread of witches and
demons, which he believed always haunted his
pathway or hid in dark corners to seize upon him
as he passed. The Thuringian forest which surrounded the town was supposed to be teeming with
evil spirits, and beneath the ground, in the mines
where Father Luther worked, was a possible dwell-
ing-place of the devil himself. Superstitious fears
thus fastened themselves upon his mind, and he had
no liberty until he found it in a saner conception of
the boundless love and limitless power of Christ.
Such was the religious atmosphere which young
Luther breathed. Such were the gruesome thoughts
that haunted him by night and taunted him by day.
Is it any wonder that a merciful God poured the
light into his soul, and that the light which could
dispel the darkness of that soul could also lighten
the path of millions of others who sat in darkness?

Chapter II
SCHOOL-DAYS

Martin's father longed to give his children better educational advantages than he himself had enjoyed. As Martin was the eldest son, they were especially desirous that he be well trained. Of course, strictly speaking, Martin's training began in the home at his mother's knee, but while he was still of a tender age his ambitious parents started him to the village school. It seems that Luther attended this school more or less regularly until he was thirteen years of age. When Luther met with severity in his home from the hands of his parents that severity was mellowed with an honest love. But when the timid, barefoot boy stepped over the threshold of the village school he found himself in different hands. Here he met severity without love. Doubtless Luther had some good teachers in school, but frequently he suffered at the hands of those who were brutal and ignorant. He received fifteen whippings at school during one forenoon. This was not because he was so mean, but because his teacher was ignorant. The lower schools throughout Germany at that time were hardly worthy of the name "school," and Luther compared them to "hell and purgatory."

14

Martin Luther as a boy did not appreciate such
a school as it was his lot to attend, but he was not
allowed to quit, for his parents had an honest ambition that he should be educated to become a lawyer. In this direction they bent every effort, but
they were greatly disappointed, as we shall see
later, when Luther decided to leave all worldly
occupations to enter upon a strictly religious life.
So Luther went on to the village school, studied
his Latin, received his whippings, and hated his
teachers until he was thirteen years of age. A
thousand wonders it is that he did not become disgusted with teachers, books, and beating-rods,
run away from home, and become an outlaw.
Think what it would have meant to the world if
he had done so. But perhaps in these trying days
he read the life of some great man, as you are
doing, and his soul must have been set ablaze with
an ambition to become educated and good, so that
he might be able to accomplish something worth
while in the world. Therefore, he continued his
studies. It is easy to imagine that young Luther
had two burning ambitions—one to become wise
and the other to become good—because he later
became both, and he could hardly have become so
without such ambitions. If a young man would

find the greatest blessing in the world let him go in search of righteousness; if he would find the next greatest blessing in the world let his search be for knowledge. Luther sought and found them both. If a young man would shun the greatest curse in the world let him shun sin; if he would shun the next greatest curse in the world let him shun ignorance. As a young man Luther shunned both.

When the schoolmasters at Mansfeld were through pounding Latin into Luther with a stick he was ready for a well-earned promotion. So about the time that Columbus was getting ready to make his third trip to America, Luther was getting ready to make his first trip to school away from home. This trip of Luther's took him to Magdeburg, a town located on the Elbe River about forty miles from his home. He was accompanied to Magdeburg by another lad from Mansfeld. Little is known as to what subjects the reformer-to-be studied while at Magdeburg, but more is known as to how he paid his expenses. The school that Luther attended at Magdeburg was a religious school managed by pious persons who exacted no tuition of Luther, because of his poverty. Young Luther, though freed from tuition expense, was confronted with the problem of meeting his personal expenses by starting with an empty purse.

But when a young man is determined to have an education he generally gets it even though he has to conquer poverty to do so. Though poor in purse Luther was rich in natural gifts. He had a good pair of legs to carry him from house to house and a strong voice to sing when he arrived. It was common, during his stay in Magdeburg, to see him with a group of fellow students as poor as himself, standing at the front gate of a wealthy citizen singing for their breakfast. Sometimes they were invited to come in, sit at the table, and eat with those to whom they sang. Sometimes with eager hands they received "handouts" at the door. The young student of the present day who has to do janitor work or wash dishes in order to pay his school expenses should extract comfort from the fact that he is following in the footprints of one of the world's greatest figures—only he uses his hands whereas Luther used his lungs.

During his stay in Magdeburg Luther was profoundly impressed with the strict piety that prevailed in connection with school-life there. Thirty-five years after he had attended this school he wrote: "When, in my fourteenth year, I went to school at Magdeburg, I saw with my own eyes a prince of Anhalt . . . who went in a friar's cowl [a hooded garment] on the highway to beg bread, and carried a sack, like a donkey, so heavy that he bent under it, but his companion walked by him without a burden; this prince alone might serve as an example of the grisly, shorn holiness of the world. They had so stunned him that he did all the works of the cloister like any other brother, and he had so fasted, watched, and mortified his flesh, that he looked like a death's head, mere skin and bones; indeed he soon after died, for he could not long bear such a severe life. In short, whoever looked at him had to gasp for pity and must needs be ashamed of his own worldly position." Luther had seen the prince he here describes in the days when his boyish mind was filled with the philosophy of the ascetic. In those days he had been taught and led to believe that the favor of God was bought by physical self-abasement. To behold such an example would naturally impress him with the thought that this prince had a high degree of righteousness.

When Luther had sung in the streets and studied in the school at Magdeburg for scarcely one year his stay in that city came to an end. Eisenach was a city twenty-five miles farther from Luther's home than was Magdeburg. In that city was a school known as the School of St. George. This was the native town of Martin's mother, and she had a relative living there, named Hutter. Perhaps Mrs. Luther had hopes that her son Martin could live with this relative and thus avoid the necessity of begging his way as he was forced to do in Magdeburg. In this she was mistaken, for Martin had no sooner landed in the city than the clear notes of his song were lifted on the breeze of the morning, and there he begged bread for his body while in search of bread for his mind. Doubtless he became very much downcast at times; he may have been tempted to return home to Mansfeld to go into the dark mines and there spend his life toiling beside his father. But it is a long and dreary song that has no ending and Martin's singing one day came to a happy termination.

In the city of Eisenach lived a woman of beautiful character—Ursula Cotta. She had often seen the poor Luther boy in the streets and had heard the clear note of his song. She had eyes that saw and a heart that pitied. She saw in the neglected boy qualities of great worth and she pitied him in his poverty. She and her husband, Conrad, invited the poor lad to come into their beautiful home and share its comforts. This event was the dawning of a new and bright day in Luther's life. It was the first time in all his career that he had felt the soft touch of refined sympathy. He spent about

Luther Invited Into the Cottas' Home

20

four years in this stately old house, by some identified with one still standing, which is visited annually by thousands of people who know of the great work of the Reformer and who bless the memory of the woman who helped him in his hour of deep need.

Luther's stay in the city of Eisenach was indeed a happy one. He referred to the city in later life as "that dear city." He entered heart and soul into his studies in the school of St. George. He stored his mind with rich gems of thought, and drank deeply of the spirit of piety possessed by his teachers. In this school Martin came into contact with the great currents of thought that were being poured forth by the intellectuals as a result of their researches into old and neglected libraries and museums.

At the close of his four years' happy residence in the Cotta home, Luther made preparation to enter the famous university of Erfurt, about twenty miles east of Eisenach. By this time his father at Mansfeld, by dint of hard labor and simple honesty, had brought himself to a place of comparative financial and social comfort. He had been placed in one of the highest offices of his village. He was still ambitious for the educational success of his son, and gave him all possible assistance in entering the great university. About May of 1501 Luther enrolled as a student at Erfurt. It seems that he remained at this center of learning for about four years, during which time he threw himself ambitiously into a study of the curriculum provided by the university. Not a great deal is known of the life of the future reformer during his university days. He lived a life of strict morality, and suffered somewhat from depression and some illness. In 1502 he took the degree of bachelor of arts and three years later that of master of arts.

It will be seen that Luther spent about nine years in training after he had left the lower school in Mansfeld before he entered upon what he at that time supposed to be his life-work—that of a monk. He was able to use the information gained in these years of schooling later in life, when he was called upon to combat the works and workers of unrighteousness in high places.

CHAPTER III
A GREAT BATTLE

The life of Luther was a life of battles. Perhaps he never shouldered a musket, or unsheathed a sword, or operated a machine gun, but his weapons of warfare were not carnal. The greatest battles of life are fought within one's own soul. From early childhood Luther had been haunted by fears that God's wrath was being stored up against him. He felt sure that God was angry with him, and he lived in constant dread of the judgment-day. Now, during the latter years of his university career he was afraid that he might die suddenly and then he would be eternally damned. "What must I do to be saved?" was the question of questions in his heart. If he had ever read the Bible with an understanding the answer would have come sweet and clear, 'Believe on the Lord Jesus Christ, Luther, and you shall be saved.' But the Bible to him was a closed book. He read it more or less, but like Saul of Tarsus he was blinded by the scales on his eyes. He did not look to the Bible for an answer to his burning question. He had been taught to look to the Roman Catholic Church for the answer. The Church replied, "Do good works, do penance, humiliate yourself, shut

23

yourself away from the world as much as possible, and you shall be saved." Luther believed the Church. It advised him to become a monk if he would be perfect and have great reward in heaven.

But what is a monk? A monk in Luther's day was a man who had become so good (according to his own idea of goodness) that he was good for nothing. He was a man who had retired from secular life to give himself entirely to religious duties. And this religious work was to be centered upon himself. He was to make himself holy, not by faith in Jesus, by which one serves his fellow men and tries to bring others to Jesus, but by prayers, and fastings, and self-humiliation. He was to vow that he would not marry, that he would remain in poverty, and that he would obey the rules of the monkish order to which he belonged. He was supposed to live in a monastery with other monks as useless to his fellow men as himself, and to spend his days in keeping himself fit to go to heaven when he died. All of this is what the Church told Martin Luther he must do to be saved. Luther, of course, wanted to be saved, but he did not want to do all this. So here is where the battle began.

All through his years in the university this struggle went on in his heart. "What must I do to be saved?" "Shall I be lost forever, or shall I obey the voice of the church?" "Shall I give up hopes of a brilliant career in secular life?" "Shall I become a monk and be scoffed at by all my young university associates, and bring down upon my youthful head the hot wrath of my poor old father, who has worked so hard that I might have an education?" All of these questions, with others equally baffling, surged through his mind.

When Luther was in the midst of this struggle certain happenings in Erfurt seemed to warn him that he was near the gates of eternity. The plague broke out in the city; many of the students died, and others, panic-stricken, fled from the place. In the face of these happenings, Luther became more solemn than ever. He tried to listen to the professors of law lecture, but their lectures were insufferably dry and uninteresting to him. What cared he for the long-drawn-out discourses of technical law when his soul was yearning for an assurance that it was saved? He left the university and went home, perhaps for the purpose of persuading his father to let him give up his study of law. But we have no reason to believe that his father consented. On July 2 as he was returning to the university he was overtaken by a severe thunder-storm. The rain came down in torrents, the wind blew, the heavens were black, the thunder roared, and angry streaks of lightning flashed. The young master of philosophy was stricken with horror. He thought the devil was actually after him. If it seems strange that a university student should get frightened at a thunder-storm we have only to recall that a belief in the direct intervention of Satan was prominent in the thought of that day. Luther fell on his face and prayed, not to God, but to St. Anna, for he believed that he could not come direct to the heavenly Father in his prayers, but that some departed saint must intercede for him. Here he made a vow that he would become a monk. The battle was over.

A few days later he invited a group of his fellow students to a social gathering. Here they feasted, sang, and had a jolly good time. Young Luther seemed to enjoy himself immensely with his friends, among whom he was a favorite, for he was a young man of high intellectuality, and many pleasing qualities. In the midst of the gayety he broke the news of his decision to his friends in these words, "Friends, today you see me for the last time; I have decided to become a monk." They believed him to be joking. When they were finally assured that he was in dead earnest they did everything in their power to pull him away from his purpose, but they were unsuccessful.

That very night he went to the convent or monastery where he disappeared behind the great cloister doors. The monastery which Luther entered was conducted by the Augustinian order of friars. There were several others in Erfurt. Luther entered this one because it had a reputation for being the best. If it were the best, pity the worst! Luther had not been in this convent very long until he found that some of the monks were not in any sense good people. Some, like Luther, doubtless had entered the convent in the hope of becoming good. But many of them, instead of growing good, had grown worse and were not ashamed of it. Some were idle, gluttonous and lazy—enormous fellows with red noses, showing that they were more interested in wine and sausages than in religion. Some of these impious monks made life miserable for Luther. They scoffed at his serious concern for his soul.

Luther was sent by the convent authorities into the streets of the city to beg. As he had grown weary of begging during his school-days at Magdeburg and Eisenach, he did not relish it here. But there were two reasons, according to the fat monks' way of thinking, why he should beg—first, his begging brought a supply of eatables to them in the convent; secondly, begging helped Luther to be humble. It brought a physical blessing to the monks and a spiritual blessing to Luther himself.

The dismal life of the convent told upon Luther's health. He refused to eat, until he wasted away, and became mere skin and bones. Finally, the vicar-general, or manager of the convent, Staupitz, who was a kindly German, noticed Luther's sad condition and took an interest in him. He encouraged Luther to trust Jesus as his Savior, telling him that God was not angry with him, but that Luther was angry with himself. Later Luther wrote, "If Dr. Staupitz, or rather God through Dr. Staupitz, had not helped me out of my trials I would have drowned in them and would have been in hell long ago."

When Luther's father heard that he had become a monk, his wrath knew no bounds. He did everything in his power to persuade his son to leave off such a course, but to no avail. Martin was ordained a priest, in February, 1507. When he celebrated his first mass in the following May, he invited his father to attend. The father came, with some of his friends, and presented his son with a beautiful present. It seems that by this time he had softened somewhat, but not altogether. Martin thought to take advantage of this occasion, and tried to explain to his father that he had chosen a wise and noble course, but his father only replied, "Have you not heard that a man should honor his parents?"

Up at Wittenberg, about seventy miles east and about sixty miles north of Erfurt, was a new university. It had been founded about six years previously by the Elector of Saxony for the purpose of teaching the philosophy of Aristotle. Wittenberg was a much smaller and less attractive town than handsome Erfurt, but it was to be a prominent name in the world's history. About a year and a half after he was ordained a priest, Luther was invited to this new university of Wittenberg to become a lecturer on moral philosophy.

CHAPTER IV

A SAD DISAPPOINTMENT

While Martin Luther was lecturing at Wittenberg University, there came a happy day into his life. It was on this wise: there arose a dispute between several monasteries over which Staupitz had charge. The dispute grew fiercer, until it became plain that some one must go to Rome to lay the matter before the Pope for his decision. Luther, being a man of acute mentality, powerful language, and talent for discussion, and one who could be relied upon to carry a clear and honest report to the Pope, and bring a like report from him, received the appointment to accompany the agent of the aggrieved monasteries, John von Mecheln of Nuremberg. Now, the reader, by all means, must not forget what Rome meant to the devout Catholic of Luther's day. To him, the name Rome stood for everything that was worthy, and good, and holy. Rome was the habitation of His Holiness the Pope. She was the hub and center of nearly everything pious.

It must have been with a joyous heart that Luther and his companion set out for Rome on a beautiful day in October, in the year 1510. But the trip from Erfurt, Germany, to Rome, Italy, proved to be no very easy one. It was

not just a few hours' pleasant ride in a soft-cush-
ioned automobile over smooth roads. No, indeed,
it was a long, hard journey of several hundred
miles over rugged mountains, a c r o s s swollen
streams, and through dismal swamps. They went
afoot, in single file. At one time during the trip,
they were in such bad circumstances for want of
food and drink that Luther feared that they might
never live to view the holy sights in Rome. In
after years, he related the incident thus: "On the
journey to Rome the brother with whom I was
traveling and I were very tired one night and slept
with open windows until about six o'clock. When we
awoke, our heads were full of vapors, so that we
could only go four or five miles that day, tormented
by thirst and yet sickened by the wine and desiring
only the water which is deadly there. At length
we were refreshed by two pomegranates with which
excellent fruit God saved our lives."

Although the journey was long and hard, and
the travelers were weary and footsore, Luther's
pious heart was encouraged by the thought that if
they kept it up he would be repaid for all his
hardships when his glad eyes would at last view
the Holy City. After several weeks of this tire-
some journey over mountains and plains and
through cities and towns, they beheld from the

summit of a hill near by the domes and spires of the far-famed city on the Tiber. The sight was almost more than Luther's religious heart could stand. He fell on his face to the ground, and exclaimed, "Hail, Holy Rome!" Just a few miles more and he actually placed his glad feet on the streets of the Eternal City.

Luther spent four weeks in seeing the sights of the great city. They were not four weeks of unalloyed joy, as he had imagined that they might be. He had dreamed of the city as a city of saints. He had a wonderful idea of the holiness of Rome. Here was the seat of the pope, who was supposed to represent Christ, on earth. Here were the buildings, the streets, and other places made sacred by the patronage of saints. Instead of finding the city filled with an atmosphere of holiness and piety, as he had expected to find it, he found an atmosphere of worldliness and even vice. He heard stories of the very corrupt life of Alexander VI, who had been pope until about seven years before Luther's visit. He heard priests and others high in church circles speak lightly of things that the church held sacred. They even poked fun at those who were trying to live holy lives. All this caused Luther's heart to bow down with grief, and when he left Rome to go back to his home in Germany, he could scarcely bear up under his disappointment. He quoted a current saying, "If there is a hell, Rome is built over it."

When in the Holy City, Luther was very anxious to visit the chapel Sancta Sanctorum, in which was a flight of twenty-eight stair-steps. These steps were said to have been taken from the judgment-hall of Pilate, in Jerusalem. Devout Catholics thought it a very religious thing to climb these steps. They thought it would make them good, and assure forgiveness of sins. Hundreds of thousands of people from different parts of the world had dragged themselves up this staircase on their knees. Pope Leo IV in the ninth century had promised forgiveness of sins nine years, for every step a pilgrim would climb, on his knees. The pilgrim was to repeat certain prayers as he climbed. Martin Luther in all probability felt sure that this meritorious act would give him peace of soul. So (according to the account, as related later by Luther's son, Paul) on his knees he started up, but as he went up he could not feel any better. He had enough common sense, when he came to think, to realize that merely climbing stair-steps would not and could not take away his sins. As he was slowly dragging up those famous steps something kept ringing in his ears. What was it? It was a passage of Scripture that he had read when he was lecturing on the Bible in the university at Wittenberg. The verse is found in the Book of Romans and reads, "The just shall live by faith." This Scripture brought a light into the soul of Luther that was to be shed over the whole world. It was God speaking to an honest soul. When Luther heard this voice, he was done with climbing holy stair-steps on his knees. He was beginning to see that faith in Jesus Christ and in his divine power will save, and bring peace to the soul, when climbing so-called holy-steps fails.

The whole world is indebted to Luther for bringing to light the great doctrine of salvation by faith. "Save yourself by good works," had been the cry for many generations! To be sure, good works were all right, Luther granted. But works were not enough. There was nothing in making holy pilgrimages and in kissing the pope to save a poor sinner. He may climb holy stair-steps until exhausted, and remain a sinner still. If a sinner is to gain salvation, and thereby life eternal, he must do so through living faith in the blood of the crucified Savior. "Faith! Faith! Faith!" was Luther's cry. It was through living faith that this monk found peace to his own troubled soul; and it was the lost doctrine of faith in Christ that he restored to the world.

Chapter V

AN ACT THAT STARTLED THE WORLD

Luther had been a lecturer at Wittenberg University before he made the journey to Rome, but he was not made a regular professor until his return. The University was still a rather new institution, having been founded in 1502 by Frederick, called the Wise, who was elector or ruler of that part of Germany. Not a great while after his return from Rome, Luther became professor of theology in this new university. He considered this his main work. Luther was a constant student. He put in a great deal of time in hard study, but he was also a man of the people. He took active part in practical, every-day affairs. He kept in touch with the political, religious, and social questions of the times, and tried to use his learning for the betterment of these departments of life. This proved a great blessing to Luther, as well as to others. When we help others to happiness, we help ourselves to peace; hence, it seems that during Luther's work as a professor, the struggles of his own soul came to an end. He learned to trust in Jesus as his Savior.

Just whether or not he was converted at this time, we may not be able to say; perhaps he had the true faith before this time, but, at any rate, he seems to have reached a place where he understood more about the abounding love of God. It was during this period that he wrote to a brother in the church: "I should be very glad to know what is the state of your soul. Have you learned to despise your own righteousness, and put your trust in the righteousness of Christ alone? Many do not know the righteousness of God which is given us abundantly and freely in Christ, but they endeavor to do good works and depend on their own effort, their own virtues, their own merits. You were full of this great error when you were here, and I was full of it. Even now I must fight against it, and have not finished. Therefore, my beloved brother, learn Christ and him crucified. Learn to despair of thyself and to say to him, 'Thou, Lord Jesus, art my righteousness, but I am thy sin. Thou hast assumed what was mine, and given me what was thine.'"

While Luther was a professor at the University of Wittenberg, there came to the next town a strange preacher, or perhaps we should call him a peddler rather than a preacher. His name was John Tetzel. He was an agent of the Pope of Rome. The Pope was building a great church in the Holy City, and needed more money than was

coming in the regular way; so he sent Tetzel up
into Germany to sell indulgences everywhere. He
gathered up great piles of money in this way for
the Pope, and, of course, he kept plenty for himself. Great crowds of people attended his meetings
and gladly poured out their money for the indulgences. But what were indulgences? They were
promises of the pope to forgive sins. For instance,
if a man had committed so many sins, he could pay
a certain amount of money and those sins would be
forgiven. The indulgence was simply a written
statement of this forgiveness. As Tetzel wanted
to get all the money he could, he offered indulgences, not only for the sins the people had already
committed, but also for those sins which they should
commit in the future. Not only so, but a man could
pay so much money and his dead relatives would
be rescued from purgatory, or the supposed place
of temporary punishment.

Tetzel claimed to be a wonderful man. He
said that he was even much greater than St. Peter
himself. He told the people that, as soon as their
money rattled in the collection-chest, their friends
were lifted out of purgatory. So it would be a
hard-hearted fellow indeed who would not throw
in a few coins to save a poor dead friend or relative from torment. Tetzel used burning words in

picturing to the poor people the tortures of those in purgatory, and he bewailed the sheer meanness of a man who was not kind-hearted enough to pay a little money to save a soul from such torture. Of course, it would be unfair to say that all Catholics believed in such a corrupt way to get money. It is well known that Tetzel was a man unworthy even of the Roman Catholic religion.

When Martin Luther heard of the high-handed doing of this Tetzel his pious soul was filled with righteous wrath. He determined to do what he could to keep the poor people from being deceived and robbed of their money. He longed that the people might know the truth, for by this time he had learned that it is truth, and not tradition, that makes people free. This is when Luther wrote out his famous ninety-five theses. These theses were simply written propositions, or statements questioning or condemning certain beliefs and practises of the church. They virtually denied the power of the pope to forgive sin. They condemned Tetzel's method of selling indulgences, and declared that the people should be taught that if the Pope knew of the extortions of the preachers of indulgences he would rather the great church which was being built at Rome with the indulgence

money would be in ashes than be paid for in any
such way.

On Oct. 31, 1517, there was a great gathering
of the people at Wittenberg. It was on the day
preceding what was known as the Feast of All
Saints. A crowd of people had already gathered
to look upon a collection of sacred relics which the
Elector had gathered and which were displayed
at this festival. At noon of this day preceding the
Feast, Luther walked to the Wittenberg church,
and nailed a set of his ninety-five theses to the
wooden church-door. This day may be said to
be the day when the great Lutheran Reformation
began. Of course, for many years in different
countries of Europe the principle of reformation
had been taking hold, but now the issue became
clear-cut in Germany, and people began to take
sides either for or against the lion-hearted reformer.
But when Luther walked to the church that day
and tacked up his statements he never dreamed of
what a stir they would cause. He merely meant
that they should be read by those who could understand Latin, for they were written in that language. He intended that these statements should
be debated in the university. He little thought
that the common crowd at Wittenberg would take
such an interest in them. However, that paper on

Luther Nailing the Theses to the Church-Door
40

the church door expressed the very same feeling that existed, not only in Luther's mind, but also in the minds of tens of thousands of people in Germany, and in all Europe. Those who could read them in Latin explained them to those who could not understand Latin, and soon the news flew everywhere that there was a German professor at Wittenberg who was bold enough to oppose the church. Within four weeks the news had reached Pope Leo X at Rome, and soon Luther's name was a household word in all Europe.

Among the theses, or propositions, are the following:

1. Our Lord and Master Jesus Christ in saying "Penitentiam agite" [which might equally well mean "Repent ye"], meant that the whole life of the faithful should be repentance.

2. And these words cannot refer to penance— that is, confession and satisfaction.

5. The pope does not wish, nor is he able, to remit any penalty except what he or the canon law has imposed.

6. The pope is not able to remit any guilt except by declaring it forgiven by God—or in cases reserved to himself . . .

11. The erroneous opinion that canonical pen-

ance and punishment in purgatory are the same assuredly seems to be a tare sown while the bishops were asleep.

21. Therefore those preachers of indulgences err who say that a papal pardon frees a man from all penalty and assures his salvation.

22. The greater part of the people will be deceived by this undistinguishing and pretentious promise of pardon which cannot be fulfilled.

26. The pope does well to say that he frees souls from purgatory not by the power of the keys (for he has no such power) but by the method of prayer.

28. It is certain that avarice is fostered by the money chinking in the chest but to answer the prayers of the church is in the power of God alone.

29. Who knows whether all the souls in purgatory want to be freed? . . .

30. None is sure of the sincerity of his contrition, much less his full pardon.

31. They who believe themselves made sure of salvation by papal letters will be eternally damned along with their teachers.

33. One should beware of them who say that those pardons are an inestimable gift of the pope by which man is reconciled to God.

36. Every Christian truly repentant has full remission of guilt and penalty even without letters of pardon.

37. Every true Christian, alive or dead, participates in all the goods of Christ and the church without letters of pardon.

38. Nevertheless papal pardons are not to be despised.

40. True contrition seeks and loves punishment, and makes relaxations of it hateful, at least at times.

43. Christians are to be taught that he who gives to the poor or lends to one in need does better than he who buys indulgences.

50. Christians are to be taught that if the pope knew the exactions of the preachers of indulgences he would rather have St. Peter's church in ashes than have it built with the flesh and bones of his sheep.

60. The treasury of the church is the power of the keys given by Christ's merit.

62. The true treasure of the church is the holy gospel of the glory and grace of God.

71. Who speaks against the apostolic truth of indulgences, let him be anathema.

72. But who opposes the lust and license of the preachers of pardons, let him be blessed.

82. Why does not the pope empty purgatory from charity?

92. Let all those prophets depart who say to the people of Christ, "Peace, peace," where there is no peace.

93. But all those prophets do well who say to the people of Christ, "Cross, cross," and there is no cross.

Luther wrote a letter to Albert, Archbishop of Mayence, on the same day he posted his theses, which still further explains the stand he took.

"Wittenberg, October 31, 1517

"Grace and the mercy of God and whatever else may be and is!

"Forgive me, Very Reverend Father in Christ, and illustrious Lord, that I, the offscouring of men, have the temerity to think of a letter to your high mightiness. . . .

"Papal indulgences for the building of St. Peter's are hawked about under your illustrious sanction. I do not now accuse the sermons of the preachers who advertise them, for I have not seen the same, but I regret that the people have conceived about them the most erroneous ideas. Forsooth these unhappy souls believe that if they buy letters of pardon they are sure of their salvation; likewise that souls fly out of purgatory as soon as money is cast into the chest; in short, that the grace conferred is so great that there is no sin whatever which cannot be absolved thereby, even if, as they say, taking an impossible example, a man should violate the mother of God. They also believe that indulgences free them from all penalty and guilt.

"My God! thus are the souls committed, Father, to your charge, instructed unto death, for which you have a fearful and growing reckoning to pay. . . .

"What else could I do, excellent Bishop and illustrious Prince, except pray your Reverence for the sake of the Lord Jesus Christ to take away your Instructions to the Commissioners altogether and impose some other form of preaching on the proclaimer of pardons, lest perchance someone should at length arise and confute them and their Instructions publicly, to the great blame of your Highness. This I vehemently deprecate, yet I fear it may happen unless the grievance is quickly redressed. . . .

"Your unworthy son,

"Martin Luther, Augustinian, Dr. Theol."

Accompanying the despatch of his theses to Pope Leo X, Luther sent the following letter:

"To the Most Blessed Father, Leo. X. Martin

Luther, Augustinian friar, wisheth everlasting welfare.

"I have heard evil reports about myself, most blessed Father, by which I know that certain friends have put my name in very bad odor with you and yours, saying that I have attempted to belittle the power of the keys and of the Supreme Pontiff. Therefore I am accused of heresy, apostasy, and perfidy, and am called by six hundred other names of ignominy. My ears shudder and my eyes are astounded. But the one thing in which I put my confidence remains unshaken—my clear and quiet conscience. Moreover, what I hear is nothing new. With such like decorations I have been adorned in my own country by those same honorable and truthful men, i.e., by the men whose own conscience convicts them of wrong doing, and who are trying to put their own monstrous doings off on me, and to glorify their own shame by bringing shame to me. But you will deign blessed Father, to hear the true case from me, though I am but an uncouth child.

"It is not long ago that the preaching of the Jubilee indulgences was begun in our country, and matters went so far that the preachers of indulgences, thinking that the protection of your name made anything permissible, ventured openly to teach the most impious and heretical doctrines, which threatened to make the power of the Church a scandal and a laughing-stock, as if the decretals de abusionibus quaestorum did not apply to them.

"Not content with spreading this poison of theirs by word of mouth, they published tracts and scattered them among the people. In these books—to say nothing of the insatiable and unheard of avarice of which almost every letter in them vilely smells—they laid down those same impious and heretical doctrines, and laid them down in such wise that confessors were bound by their oath to be faithful and insistent in urging them upon the people. I speak the truth, and none of them can hide himself from the heart thereof. The tracts are extant and they cannot disown them. These teachings were so successfully carried on, and the people, with their false hopes, were sucked so dry that, as the Prophet says, 'they plucked their flesh from off their bones'; but they themselves meanwhile were fed most pleasantly on the fat of the land.

"There was just one means which they used to quiet opposition, to wit, the protection of your name, the threat of burning at the stake, and the disgrace of the name 'heretic.' It is incredible how ready they are to threaten, even at times, when they perceive that it is only their own mere silly opinions which are contradicted. As though this were to quiet opposition, and not rather to arouse schisms and seditions by sheer tyranny!

"None the less, however, stories about the avarice of the priests were bruited in the taverns, and evil was spoken of the power of the keys and of the Supreme Pontiff, and as evidence of this, I could cite the common talk of this whole land. I truly confess that I was on fire with zeal for Christ, as I thought, or with the heat of youth, if you prefer to have it so; and yet I saw that it was not in place for me to make any decrees or to do anything in these matters. Therefore I privately admonished some of the prelates of the Church. By some of them I was kindly received, to others I seemed ridiculous, to still others something worse; for the terror of your name, and the threat of Church censures prevailed. At last, since I could do nothing else, it seemed good that I should offer at least a gentle resistance to them, i.e., question and discuss their teachings. Therefore I published a set of theses, inviting only the more learned to dispute with me if they wished; as should be evident, even to my adversaries, from the preface to the disputation.

"Lo, this is the fire with which they complain that

all the world is now ablaze. Perhaps it is because they are indignant that I, who by your own apostolic authority am a Master of Theology, have the right to conduct public disputations, according to the custom of all the universities and of the whole Church, not only about indulgences, but also about God's power and remission and mercy, which are incomparable greater subjects. I am not much moved, however, by the fact that they envy me the privilege granted me by the power of your Holiness, since I am unwillingly compelled to yield to them in things of greater moment, viz., when they mix the dreams of Aristotle with theological matters, and conduct nonsensical disputations about the majesty of God, beyond and against the privilege granted them.

"It is a miracle to me by what fate it has come about that this single disputation of mine should, more than any other, of mine or of any of the teachers, have gone out into very nearly the whole land. It was made public at our University and for our University only and it was made public in such wise that I cannot believe it has become known to all men. For it is a set of theses, not doctrines or dogmas, and they are put, according to custom, in an obscure and enigmatic way. Otherwise, if I had been able to foresee what was coming, I should have taken care, for my part, that they would be easier to understand.

"Now what shall I do? I cannot recant them; and yet I see that marvelous enmity is inflamed against me because of their dissemination. It is unwillingly that I incur the public and perilous and various judgment of men, especially since I am unlearned, dull of brain, empty of scholarship; and that too in this brilliant age of ours, which by its achievements in letters and learning can force even Cicero into the corner, though he was no base follower of the public light. But necessity compels me to be the goose that squawks among the swans.

"And so, to soften my enemies and to fulfil the desires of many, I herewith send forth these trifling explanations of my disputation; I send them forth in order, too, that I may be more safe under the defense of your name and the shadow of your protection. In them all may see, who will, how purely and simply I have sought after and cherished the power of the Church and reverence for the keys; and at the same time, how unjustly and falsely my adversaries have befouled me with so many names. For if I had been such a one as they wish to make me out, and if I had not on the contrary, done everything correctly, according to my academic privilege, the Most Illustrious Prince Frederick, Duke of Saxony, Imperial Elector, etc., would never have tolerated such a pest in his University, for he most dearly loves the Catholic and Apostolic truth, nor could I have been tolerated by the keen and learned men of our University. But what has been done, I do because those most courteous men do not fear openly to involve both the Prince and the University in the same disgrace with myself.

"Wherefore, most blessed Father, I cast myself at the feet of your Holiness, with all that I have and all that I am. Quicken, kill, call, recall, approve, reprove, as you will. In your voice I shall recognize the voice of Christ directing you and speaking in you. If I have deserved death, I shall not refuse to die. For the earth is the Lord's and the fulness thereof. He is blessed forever. Amen.

"May he have you too forever in his keeping. Amen."

Chapter VI

WHAT THE POPE THOUGHT OF LUTHER

When Pope Leo saw the theses, he was not at all alarmed. However, he was very much disgusted. When he had read them he remarked, "Oh, some drunken German has written them; as soon as he is sober again he will speak differently." Luther's friends were aware of the grave danger into which he was thrown. They knew the spirit of Rome. They remembered how that just about twenty years before this time, Savonarola had met his death in Italy, because he was bold enough to denounce Pope Alexander VI for his sins. They begged Luther to be a little more considerate of what he said. Even his former instructors in the University of Erfurt turned against him and reproached him for his insolent attacks upon the church. Some of the officials of the University begged him not to bring the institution into disgrace by giving it a reputation for being untrue to the doctrines of the church.

John Tetzel was given the doctor's degree by a neighboring university, and honors were heaped upon him in many quarters, which were done in testimony of the contempt that was held in those quarters for the reformer. But Luther's courage did not fail. He believed he was doing God's

will, and he refused to be persuaded by his friends
or frightened by his foes into giving up the work
which he felt called upon to do.

Finally, Pope Leo spoke. He ordered Luther
to come to Rome within sixty days to answer to
the charge of teaching unsound doctrine. Before
Luther could decide whether to go or not, Cardinal
Cajetan, who represented the Pope in the German
Empire, warned Leo that there was danger in al-
lowing Luther at large any longer, and requested
that he be dealt with at once, at Augsburg. Cajetan was informed that he should arrest Luther immediately.

The trial was set to be held in Augsburg before
a court of the Romish representatives. Cardinal
Cajetan had instructions to use all diligence to see
that the bold monk was brought to punishment if
he did not recant. He was instructed to threaten
with punishment, not only Luther himself, but all
who would dare to house, or shield, or in any way,
either openly or privately, protect, or assist, or
counsel the said Martin Luther.

When it became known to Luther that he must
go to Augsburg to face the charges brought against
him, it appears that he thought he would never return alive. "I must die," he said; and "Oh, the
disgrace that I heap upon my poor parents!" But,

"The Lord's will be done. Even at Augsburg, even in the midst of his enemies, Christ reigns. Let Christ live; let Luther die!" He was accompanied at Augsburg by Dr. Staupitz, and other friends, and he was guaranteed a safe-conduct by the Emperor Maximilian. When he reached Augsburg, in the month of October, he found that the council had adjourned, and most of the members departed. But he had a meeting with Cardinal Cajetan. The Cardinal talked to him with great courtesy at first, in the hope of getting him to apologize to the church and to the Pope. Luther replied that he was ready to apologize as soon as he was shown wherein he was wrong. The Cardinal said that in one of his theses Luther had claimed that the treasury of the Church consisted not of the sufferings and merits of Christ. And in his Resolutions, or explanations of his theses, he had claimed that the sacrament, or Lord's Supper, was of value only to those who had faith in the promise of God. He asked Luther to admit that he was wrong. Luther refused. The Cardinal became furious and shouted, "Go away! Revoke or do not come again before my eyes." He remarked to Dr. Staupitz, "I will no longer dispute with that beast, for it has deep eyes and wonderful speculations in its head." Luther slipped out of Augsburg by night, and made his way back to Wittenberg arriving there October 30, just one day less than a year from the day he had nailed his ninety-five theses to the church-door. The enraged Cardinal demanded that Luther should be sent in chains to Rome, but Frederick the Elector, who was determined that Luther should have a fair trial, would not allow that he be sent to Rome.

But if Cardinal Cajetan was not smooth enough to fix things up with the "beast of Wittenberg," as he called Luther, the Pope had another agent who was much smoother, and he would send him to Germany to see what could be done. This was Charles von Miltitz, who was an old resident of Rome and thoroughly familiar with her ways. He was shrewd and cultured. He soon found that there was a tremendous sentiment, in Germany, in favor of Luther's movement. He said that three persons out of every four he met were on Luther's side. Of course, he was too wise to disregard this sentiment of the common people. He had a meeting with Luther and talked matters over. He denounced Tetzel as a fraud, and agreed that Luther's case should be tried by an enlightened bishop. It was agreed by him and Luther that both sides should keep silent, and let the trouble between Luther and the Church die out. Luther agreed to write a letter to the Pope and apologize, if he had been too rough in what he had said. Miltitz was also to write to the Pope, and tell him that an adjustment had been made. So it seemed that the trouble was settled.

Luther meant to keep his word when he promised to keep quiet, and it was not his fault that he did not. Perhaps it is well that he was drawn further into the discussion, for had he remained silent perhaps we never should have had the great religious Reformation that shook the whole world. In the University of Wittenberg was a professor called Carlstadt, who was a friend of Luther's, and a believer in his doctrines. In the University of Ingolstadt was a professor named Eck, once a friend, but now an enemy of Luther, and a staunch supporter of the Church. Carlstadt came forward with a set of theses against Eck. In Eck's reply, it was very plain that while he was claiming to attack Carlstadt he in reality was attacking Luther. Luther protested that it was unfair for him to be required to keep silent when his enemies were allowed to rage. He immediately published some new theses in opposition to Eck, which brought on the debate at Leipzig. This debate lasted for three weeks. Carlstadt proved to be no match for Dr. Eck, but Luther came boldly forward the second week and defended the truth in the very face of those who were its enemies. In this debate, it became clear that the breach between Luther and the Roman Catholic Church was growing wider and wider.

In 1520, Luther wrote his famous Address to the German Nobility. This was an appeal to the German people to stand for their national rights. It called attention to the fact that the German nation was overridden by the lords of Rome, and called upon them to arise and throw off their yoke of bondage. He said it would be well if ninety-nine parts of the papal court were done away and called it "a swarm of vermin yonder in Rome" and "ravening wolves in sheep's clothing." He said in this address that the Romanists had built three walls about themselves, behind which they carried on their meanness. Luther declared his intention to hammer these three walls down and show the popes and their colleagues up in all their uncleanness. The first wall was the pope's claim that he and his emissaries were not subject to the temporal power. If threatened with the law for their misdeeds they said that the law could not touch them, for they were higher than any temporal power and were not subject to it. Strange belief to hold, we say to-day, but in Luther's day almost everybody held that belief. It had been taught for years, and even for centuries. But Luther declared that all Christians were on an equal footing in this respect, and that all were alike subject to the temporal power. Crime should be punished by the temporal power whether the criminal were pope, priest, or peasant. In his Address to the Nobility he stated that there is no difference among Christians save of office alone. Furthermore, he said that we are all Christians by a higher consecration than pope or bishop can give for the bishop's consecration is just as if, in the name of the whole congregation, he took one member out of the community, each member of which has equal power, and commanded him to exercise this power for the rest. Or it is just as though ten brothers, coheirs as king's sons, were to choose one from among them to rule over their inheritance; they would, all of them, still remain kings and have equal power, although one were ordered to govern. To make the subject clearer, he gave this illustration: If a little company of Christian laymen were taken prisoners, and carried away to a desert, and had among them no priest consecrated by a bishop, and were there to agree to choose one of them, married or unmarried, and were to order him to baptize, to celebrate the mass, to absolve, and to preach, this man would be as truly a priest as though all the bishops and all

the popes had consecrated him. A priest, therefore, said he, is nothing in Christendom but an
official. As long as he holds his office he has pre-
cedence over others; if he be deprived of it, he is
a peasant or townsman like the rest. He said a
cobbler, a smith, a peasant, every man has the
office and function of his calling, and yet all alike
they are consecrated priests and bishops, and every
man in his work must be useful and beneficial to
the rest.

Continuing, he stated that to say that the temporal authority, being inferior to the clergy, dare
not punish them, is as though one were to say that
the hand may not help when the eye is suffering.
Inasmuch as the temporal power has been ordained
of God for the punishment of the bad and the protection of the good, we must let it do its duty
throughout the whole Christian body without respect of persons, whether it strike pope, bishops,
priests, monks, nuns or anybody else. He raised
the question that if a priest is killed, the country is
laid under an interdict—why not, also, if a peasant
is killed?

So Luther crumbled the first wall. Now for the
second wall. This second wall that the Romanists had built around themselves to shield them in
their meanness was the idea that the pope was the

only one who could interpret the Scripture correctly. If a pope or a priest did any evil and was threatened by the Scriptures it was easy enough for the pope to interpret the Bible in a way to suit himself, and when his Holiness said a certain scripture meant a certain thing everybody must keep silent, for according to the generally accepted theory he could not make a mistake. So the people kept silent and the pope kept sinning. But Luther would not keep silent. He spent months and months in searching the Scriptures, and reading church history, and the more he searched, and the more he read, the more he believed that the whole idea of the pope's infallibility was a sham and a fraud. Listen to what he says: "The second wall is still more flimsy and worthless. They wish to be the only masters of the Holy Scriptures, even though in all their lives they learn nothing from them. They assume for themselves sole authority, and with insolent juggling of words they would persuade us that the pope, whether he be a bad man or a good man, can not err in matters of faith; and yet they can not prove a single letter of it. . . . Unless I had read it myself, I could not have believed that the devil would make such clumsy pretensions at Rome, and find a following.

"But not to fight them with mere words, we will

quote the Scriptures. St. Paul says in 1 Corinthians 14: 'If to any one something better is revealed, though he be sitting and listening to another in God's Word, then the first, who is speaking, shall hold his peace and give place.' . . . Thus it may well happen that the pope and his followers are wicked men, and no true Christians, not taught of God, not having true understanding. On the other hand, an ordinary man may have true understanding; why then should we not follow him?" . . . "They must confess that there are pious Christians among us, who have the true faith, Spirit, understanding, word and mind of Christ. Why, then, should we reject their word and understanding and follow the pope, who has neither faith nor Spirit? . . . Balaam's ass also, was wiser than the prophet himself. If God thus spoke by an ass against a prophet, why should he not be able even now to speak by a righteous man against the pope?" So down comes the second wall.

Yet, there is the third. The pope believed in self-security. He claimed that he was not subject to temporal powers, but that he was subject to the Scriptures only, with his own interpretation. Now, the third wall was that he held a council illegal unless it was called, or confirmed, by himself. So he was beyond the reach of king or emperor; he was beyond the reach of the Bible; he was beyond the reach of a council. There is a scripture in Matt. 18:15, 16, 17, which says: "Moreover, if thy brother shall trespass against thee, go and tell him his fault between thee and him alone; if he shall hear thee, thou hast gained thy brother. But, if he will not hear thee, then take with thee one or two more, . . . if he shall neglect to hear them, tell it unto the church: but if he neglect to hear the church, let him be unto thee as a heathen man and a publican." Luther, in commenting on this text, said, "Here, every member is commanded to care for every other. How much rather should we do this when the member that does evil is a ruling member, and by his evil-doing is the cause of much harm and offense to the rest! But if I am to accuse him before the Church, I must bring the Church together." Note here that Luther claimed that the humblest member of the church had a right to call a council to consider the deeds of a member who had committed offense. Imagine how the pope would consider such a wide departure from the papal idea!

After Luther had smashed the three hypocritical walls that for four hundred years and more had been built up around popery, and had discussed a number of abuses that Rome had for generations perpetrated on the German people, he then proceeded to mention twenty-seven reforms that should be carried out. Some of these proposed reforms were so radical and so startling that I must here mention a few of them.

1. *Proposal Number One.*—The German people should refuse to pay annates to the pope. By the term "annates," we mean a certain form of ecclesiastical taxation, whereby the pope exacted certain gifts from his subjects, which gifts he used to satisfy his own appetite for worldly pleasure. Luther accused the papists of bold robbery, and demanded that the German people no longer tolerate the system.

2. *Proposal Number Four.*—Luther demanded that no matter of dispute of a temporal nature should be taken to Rome, but that all such cases should be left to the temporal authorities. He agreed that matters of spiritual concern may be properly laid before the pope, but he claimed that it was unscriptural for his Holiness to meddle in temporal affairs. Those things that concern money, property, life, and honor must be settled by temporal judges.

3. *Proposal Number Seven.*—It was suggested, in Luther's seventh proposal for reform, that the pope and his court should live in less luxury.

Popes in those days lived like kings, only on a grander scale. Luther demanded that the "swarm of vermin at Rome" be diminished in number. This pompous and extravagant living by the pope, and his thousands of subordinates, meant a tremendous financial drain on the common people. Luther said that the pope's pomp should be paid for by the pope's purse. He pointed out the contrast between the grand living of the pope, and the humble living of Christ, of whom he professed to be vicar, and the apostle Peter, of whom he claimed to be successor.

4. *Proposal Number Nine.*—"The pope should have no authority over the emperor, except that he anoints and crowns him at the altar, just as a bishop anoints and crowns a king; and we should not henceforth yield to that devilish pride which compels the emperor to kiss the pope's feet or sit at his feet, or, as they claim, hold his stirrup or the bridle of his mule when he mounts for a ride; still less should he do homage and swear faithful allegiance to the pope, as the popes have shamelessly ventured to demand as if they possessed that right."

5. *Proposal Number Eleven.*—Luther thought it was silly and blasphemous for people to kiss the pope's feet, and proposed that they stop the prac-

tise. He said it was an unchristian and even antichristian thing for a pope, who was nothing but a sinful man, to allow his feet to be kissed by a man who was a hundred times better than himself. Luther compared Christ and the pope. Christ washed the disciples' feet, and wiped them with a towel, symbolizing the fact that he was their humble servant, and now here comes the pope vaunting himself as the vicar of Christ, and demanding that his subjects pay him the homage of kissing his feet. Luther could not see how "a poor stinking sinner," as he called the pope, could be worthy of such honor.

6. *Proposal Number Twelve.*—Pilgrimages to Rome should be abolished, or should be made with the consent of the town authorities. Luther held that the money spent on such pilgrimages could be more profitably used in caring for the pilgrim's family. It had frequently happened that pious and silly persons had made the journey to the Holy City, leaving their families to exist on the charity of the community at home. Such persons, even though they kissed the pope's feet times unnumbered, were, according to Luther's view, worse than infidels.

7. *Proposal Number Fourteen.*—The laws of the Romish Church forbade the marriage of her

priests. As a result of this godless demand many priests lived in open and awful adultery. Luther observed that there was many a pious priest who had been overtaken in immorality because he had vowed to the Church that he would not marry. Luther knew all this ungodly program concerning the sacred institution of matrimony to be against both divine and natural law, and he demanded that it be abolished. In closing his Address to the Nobility Luther said: "I think too that I have pitched my song in a high key, have made many propositions which will be thought impossible and have attacked many things too sharply. But what am I to do? I am in duty bound to speak. . . . I know another little song about Rome. . . . If their ears itch for it I will sing them that song too, and pitch the notes to the top of the scale. Understandest thou, dear Rome, what I mean? . . .

"Therefore, let them boldly go to work—pope, bishop, priest, monk, and scholar! They are the right people to persecute the truth, as they have ever done. God give us all a Christian mind. . . . Amen."

By the "other little song" that Luther referred to he meant his booklet on the Babylonian Captivity, in which he assailed the whole Romish system of sacraments. Later he wrote his Treatise on

Christian Liberty. Luther had now broken the last cord that bound him to the Romish Church. He had assailed her doctrines, ridiculed her practices, and defied her authority. He had done the very things for which she had burned more than one person at the stake. Would she also burn Luther? We shall see.

CHAPTER VII

LUTHER BURNS LEO'S BULL

Luther wrote and Leo raged. But Luther refused to be afraid. He said that truth was more important than his life, and that if he perished at the hands of Rome the truth which he preached would live just the same. It will be remembered that Professor Eck debated with Luther and Carlstadt, and that apparently he won the victory. He felt that he should go to Rome to tell about this victory. And to Rome he went. When he got there, of course, Pope Leo X wanted to know how Luther, the "beast of Wittenberg," was doing. And Eck reported that Luther was growing meaner as he grew older. Leo received the professor with great courtesy, and fatherly consideration. After Eck had bowed and kissed his feet, Leo surprized everybody present by kissing Eck.

Eck stayed around Rome for a while, then went back to Germany. When he went back, he went with a joyous heart, because he carried with him a bull against Luther issued by the Pope. In fact, Eck himself had assisted in drawing up the document, and on June 15, 1520, the Pope signed it. Here is a quotation from it, "Arise, O Lord, arise, judge thy cause, be mindful of the reproaches with

which the foolish reproach thee daily. Incline
thine ears to our prayers, since foxes have arisen
seeking to spoil thy vineyard—whose care, government, and administration thou didst intrust to Peter
as its head and thy vicar, and to his successors;
the boar out of the woods is seeking to waste it,
and a peculiar wild beast does devour it. Arise,
O Peter, attend to the cause of the holy Roman
Church, mother of all churches, and queen of the
faith. Arise, thou, too, O Paul! . . . Finally, let
the entire congregation of saints and the rest of the
church universal arise." In the bull were then
quoted forty-two propositions from Luther's writings. They were taken out of their regular place,
and were given a meaning that Luther in no wise
intended they should convey. It then continued,
"No one of sound mind is ignorant how poisonous,
how pernicious, how seductive to godly and simple
minds, and finally how contrary to all love and
reverence for the holy Roman Church—the founda-
tion and source of all virtue, without which every
one is proved to be an infidel—these errors are."

This bull contained several things of importance.
First, it commanded Luther to repent of all he had
said and done against the Roman Church. He
was to do this by letter if he chose, but the Pope
preferred that he should come to Rome in person,

in order that there be no doubt as to the genuineness of his submission. Secondly, the bull provided that Luther must quit preaching, teaching, and writing. Certainly, Luther would not do that. His lips insisted on speaking out the message that glowed in his heart. With Paul he could say, "Woe is me if I preach not the gospel." Thirdly, the Pope's bull demanded, not only that he cease to write, but that all his written works must be hunted, and burned to ashes. What? Burn all those precious books which defended the liberty of the people's conscience! But the Pope went still further in this communication. He pronounced all men as heretics and under the ban of excommunication who sided with Luther. These heretics were to be seized whenever possible and sent to Rome! So it may be seen at once that such a bull issued by the Church was no trivial affair.

For years and years, Rome had not failed to back up such demands, even with death itself. All those who were loyal to the Romish Church rejoiced that at last the famous document had been signed, for they were sure that it would bring about the end of the troublesome Saxon monk. And Luther's friends were sore afraid. They saw with alarm the dark clouds that were gathering thicker and blacker over Luther's head, and they feared

for the life of the brave defender of the truth.
Luther, too, knew he was in great danger, but he
trusted God to sustain him as he stood immovable
as Gibraltar.

It must not be imagined that this famous bull
passed through the Roman political and ecclesiastical machinery in a day. On the contrary it was
many weeks, and even months, in the process of
preparation. There were thousands of people who
were with Luther in his views. Pope Leo was a
man who had given himself over to carnal plea-
sures. He was more interested in the theater, the
chase, and music than he was in the promotion of
religion. Sensible men everywhere plainly saw this.
Even in Rome there were critics of Rome. There
were those who knew there was more fact than fic-
tion in what Luther had been saying about "dear
Rome." These persons contended that Luther
should be dealt with in moderation. Said they,
"Perhaps the German monk, if dealt with reason-
ably, can be saved to the church: we should take
more time for reflection." So the Pope and his
advisers were undecided. But now Dr. Eck came
forward in all his fury. He mustered all his forces.
The fanatical priests sided with him, and gave him
new courage. He said that the people in Rome
could not know the real danger of the "beast of

Wittenberg," as they were such a distance from him. Luther said, "Eck is stirring up the bottomless pit against me." Just at this time, a wealthy banker came to the aid of Eck. He urged the Pope to use every means possible to silence Luther, and promised money to aid him in his task. The papacy, always ready to receive money, was glad for the generous offer. The decision was made. Luther was condemned, if he did not retract in sixty days, and Eck was happy.

When the bull against Luther had been duly drawn up and signed, a question arose as to who should be the messenger to carry it to Germany. There were several persons around Rome who were anxious to have this distinction. In Eck's conceited mind, he himself was the proper person to carry the bull to Germany. Why should he not be? He had been the bitter enemy of Luther for years. He had disputed with him at Leipzig. He was fully aware of all the dangers to the Church that were set up in Germany. He was conceited enough, flattering enough, impudent enough, and drunken enough, to do an excellent job in carrying such a project as he was desirous of undertaking to a successful end. So against the will of many sensible men, even in Rome, he was appointed special nuncio to convey the document to

Germany. Imagine his joy and exaltation as he
left the city of the seven hills, with victory itself
in his hands. He had Luther's condemnation right
with him. Victory! Victory! Victory! was his
watchword as he crossed the Alps and made his
way into Germany.

But, was not God on his throne? Eck's pride
was soon changed to humiliation. He had expected to be received in Germany with great en-
thusiasm. However, many people were indifferent
toward the professor and his message, and more
were decidedly hostile. He had hoped to have
the bull published far and wide in Germany, but
the bishops refused to give it publicity. In certain towns where it was posted at all, it was posted
in obscure places, where it was not generally read.
Even the protector, Duke George, was not favor-
able to its publication. When full of wine Eck
displayed the bull, and boasted how he "intended
bringing that scoundrel Martin to reason." He
took lodging at Leipzig, where he suffered much
humiliation. A group of students posted up
placards in a number of places, condemning and
ridiculing Dr. Eck. Things became so warm for
him, that he fled into a cloister, where Tetzel had
formerly been in hiding, and there he refused to be
interviewed. The students composed a sarcastic

song about him, and sang where he could hear it. Eck was much cast down. A throng of students came from Luther's university and raged out against him. Eck slipped out of his hiding-place one night, and left the city. Some students at Erfurt, when copies of the bull were posted at their university, tore them down, and threw them in the river, exclaiming, "Since it is a bull [a bubble] let it float."

Eck frequently got drunk, but he always remained sober enough to stay away from Wittenberg in person. So he sent his bull there and demanded that it be published. Was it published? "I know nothing of Eck," said Luther, "except that he has arrived [from Rome] with a long beard, a long bull, and a long purse; but I laugh at his bull. . . . I despise and attack it as impious, false, and in every respect worthy of Eck. It is Christ himself who is condemned therein. No reasons are given in it. I am cited to Rome, not to be heard, but that I may eat my words. Oh, that Charles V would act like a man; and that for the love of Christ he would attack these wicked spirits. I rejoice in having to bear such ills for the best of causes. Already I feel greater liberty in my heart; for at last I know that the pope is antichrist, and that his throne is that of Satan himself." Luther wrote a tract about this time entitled "The New Bull and the Lies of Eck."

The Pope caused many of Luther's writings to be burned; Luther paid him back in his own change. When Eck sent the bull to Wittenberg, the professors refused to post it, but instead posted this notice in a public place on Monday, December 10, "All friends are invited to assemble about nine o'clock at the church of the Holy Cross outside the city walls, where the godless books of the papal constitutions and scholastic theology will be burned according to ancient and apostolic usage, inasmuch as the boldness of the enemies of the gospel has waxed so great that they have cast the godly, evangelical books of Dr. Luther into the fire. Come, pious and zealous youth, to this pious and religious spectacle, for it is now the time when the antichrist must be exposed."

When nine o'clock came a great crowd of students and professors had gathered about the university buildings. Luther himself headed the procession. They marched outside of the town, and built a bonfire. When the flames were blazing in the air, and the smoke was curling toward the sky, Luther stepped forward with the Pope's bull in his hand. Imagine if you can the serious look on every one's face, when he threw the bull into the

"He threw the bull into the flames"

flames, as he uttered these words, "Because thou hast brought down the truth of God, he also brings thee down unto this fire today. Amen." Luther returned quietly to his room, where he wrote a tract explaining why he had burned the Pope's bull. A number of students celebrated the occasion by singing songs ridiculing the Pope. They obtained a wagon, went from house to house through the city, and collecting all the Catholic books they could find piled them on the fire. Near the place where the fire was built is an oak-tree known as Luther's Oak. Every year it is visited by hundreds of tourists, who read this inscription on a tablet, "Dr. Martin Luther burned, at this place, on December 10, 1520, the papal bull."

The next day after Luther had burned the bull he lectured in the assembly-room of the university to a vast audience of students and doctors. He condemned the papacy in the hottest terms, and called upon all who were present to stand solidly for reformation. His address produced a profound effect on the students. They regarded Luther as a messenger sent of God to declare the truth, as indeed he was.

It will be remembered that the bull was dated June 15, and that it gave Luther sixty days to humble himself, and apologize to the Pope. It was nearly Christmas when Luther burned the bull. He had become more bold with the passing months. It was now very plain to Pope Leo X that Luther did not intend to revoke his theses; so on Jan. 3, 1521, he issued a final bull of excommunication in which Luther and those who followed him were cut off from the Church, and consigned to the punishment which the Church provided for heretics. So we see Luther as an outlaw under the curse of the Roman Church, the most humanly powerful religious force then on earth.   What will he do? What will become of him?   Will God forsake him?   We shall see.

Chapter VIII

LUTHER BEFORE THE EMPEROR

Germany's new emperor was just a boy—Charles V, who was only about twenty years of age. After a hot political fight he had succeeded in getting himself elected as head of the Holy Roman Empire which included the German nation. But Charles V knew and cared little about things German. He was not in sympathy with German traditions, nor German sentiment. He did not even understand the German language. There was one thing that Charles was anxious to do, and that was to keep the favor of Pope Leo X, for though he was young, he was wise enough to know that Pope Leo could have a large influence in helping him to realize any of his political ambitions.

So far as Martin Luther was concerned, Charles cared nothing for him any more than to use him, if possible, as a tool to further his own interests with the Pope. But Frederick, Elector of Saxony, was a friend to Luther, and he had great power with Charles V, for it was largely through Frederick's influence that Charles was exalted to the throne. Frederick had been offered the crown himself, but was too wise to accept it under the existing circumstances. If it had not been for

Frederick, Charles would have made things much more unpleasant for Luther than he did.

On November 17, Luther had made an appeal from the pope to a general church council, composed of the dignitaries of the church.

In January, 1521, Charles V, a few months after the day on which he was crowned, opened his first assembly of the Empire, or diet, at Worms, an old and historic city up the Rhine River. It was before this council that Luther was to stand and defend, or revoke, the books he had written against the Romish system. Pope Leo X sent to this council, as his representative, one Aleander, who is represented as a shrewd and courteous liar. He was a smooth politician, and left no stones unturned to see that Luther received the worst that Rome could give. An imperial edict was issued, upon an order from Pope Leo to Charles V that the bull of excommunication against Luther should be carried out in Germany. On it Aleander made a speech three hours long before the diet. In eloquent terms, he pleaded with the council that Luther's writings were sufficient to justify the burning of the Wittenberg monk. He insisted that Luther should not be permitted to come before the diet. He had already been condemned by the great head of the Church, the pope, and was not that sufficient?

Why waste the time of the Emperor, and princes, in listening to the babblings of a contemptible monk? But his eloquence did not win the day, and after much debate, it was decided that Luther himself should be called before the council.

It was late in March, 1521, when a messenger sent from Charles reached Luther, and informed him that he was to come before the council to furnish information concerning the books and papers he had been writing. When the messenger, accompanied by a servant reached the town of Wittenberg he found Luther in poor health, quietly at work in the University. This is the message that was carried to Luther:

"Charles, by the grace of God Emperor elect of the Romans, . . .

"Honorable, well-beloved, and pious—We and the states of the holy empire here assembled, having resolved to institute an inquiry touching the doctrine and the books that thou hast lately published, have issued, for thy coming hither, and thy return to a place of security, our safe-conduct and that of the empire, which we send thee herewith. Our sincere desire is, that thou shouldst prepare immediately for this journey, in order that within the space of twenty-one days fixed by our safe-conduct, thou mayest without fail be present before us. Fear neither injustice nor violence. We will firmly abide by our aforesaid safe-conduct, and expect that thou will comply with our summons. In so doing, thou wilt obey our earnest wishes.

"Given in our imperial city of Worms, the sixth day of March, in the year of our Lord, 1521, and the second of our reign.

"CHARLES."

Would Luther go to Worms? And what would happen to him if he went? Would the Emperor's promise of safety be kept? Had not Huss been given just such a promise of safety, when he went to the Council of Constance, and had he not been killed in spite of such a safe-conduct? What would Luther do? What would most men do in his place?

His friends were alarmed. All over Germany there was a great stir. Those who believed in the Reformation were uneasy, fearing lest the reformer, in going to Worms, was going to his death. The Elector, Frederick, Luther's great protector, expressed grave fears.

As for Luther himself, he saw the danger, but he did not fear it. He believed that God would shield him if it were his will, and if it were not his will he did not care to be shielded. We hear him at this time saying, "Fear not that I shall retract a single syllable. . . . If the Emperor summons me that I may be put to death as an enemy of the empire, I am ready to comply with his call; for with the help of Christ, I will never desert the word on the battle-field. I am well aware that these bloodthirsty men will never rest until they have taken away my life." When Elector Frederick had asked him if he were willing to come to Worms if called, he had replied, "If I am called, I shall go; and if I were too sick to go, I shall have them carry me. It were wrong to doubt that God calls me when the emperor calls." On seeing the concern of his friends for his welfare, Luther said: "The papists do not desire my coming to Worms, but my condemnation and my death. It matters not. Pray not for me, but for the word of God. Before my blood has grown cold, thousands of men in the whole world will have become responsible for having shed it. The most holy adversary of Christ, the father, the master, the generalissimo of murderers, insists on its being shed. So be it. Let God's will be done. Christ will give me his Spirit to overcome these ministers of error. I despise them during my life; I shall triumph over them by my death. They are busy at Worms about compelling me to retract; and this shall be my retraction: I said formerly that the pope was Christ's vicar; now I assert that he is our Lord's adversary and the devil's apostle."

So amidst the tears of his friends, on April 2, Luther left his beloved Wittenberg for Worms. Would he ever return? It was doubtful, very doubtful. He turned to Melanchthon, his great partner in the work, and said with a trembling voice, "My dear brother, if I do not return, and my enemies put me to death, continue to teach, and stand fast in the truth. Labor in my stead, since I shall no longer be able to labor for myself. If you survive my death will be of little consequence." Then, with three companions, he climbed into a common canvas-covered wagon, furnished by the town of Wittenberg, passed through the gates of the town, and began his journey to Worms. The distance from Wittenberg to Worms was something near three hundred miles, according to the route of travel. Luther had to pass through many towns and cities before reaching there. Everybody along the way was eager to see the man who was bold enough to oppose the whole world. They had heard of him, and now they must see him with their own eyes. In every town his path was thronged with people. Many of them hailed him as a great hero. Others insulted him as a despised nuisance. His friends feared he would be killed at Worms, and his enemies feared he would not. But in spite of friends or enemies, he would go. He said he would go if the devils in Worms were as thick as the tiles on the roofs of the houses.

When he reached the town of Naumburg, he met a certain priest. This priest had a picture of Savonarola, who had been condemned to death in Italy by Pope Alexander VI, and was burned for trying to do the very same thing Luther was trying to do—reform the Church. This priest took this picture down from the wall of his study-room, and walking toward Luther, held it up before his eyes, without saying a word. This priest was a friend of Luther's work, and he meant this act as a silent warning to him of what the Church did to those who opposed her. But it would take more than the pictures of martyrs to scare this bold German monk. So went he on his journey, and when he drew near the city of Erfurt, where he had attended school, and had sung for something to eat, in the gloomy days of his youth, he was met by a large group of horsemen who had come out to welcome him. These were leading men of the city and University at Erfurt, and they had made arrangements for Luther to speak to a great crowd of people at a church while there. When they left Erfurt, he and his three traveling companions were joined by three or four persons who journeyed on with them to Worms. One of these new companions was a young lawyer by the name of Justus Jonas who, from that time on, came to be a close friend and helper of Luther in the work of the Reformation.

As the days and hours brought Luther and his company nearer and nearer Worms, all was excitement. The news of their coming went before them. His enemies would have made away with him but for the King's safe-conduct. Luther sent word to a friend of his, who was at Worms, to prepare lodging for him. On the morning of April 16, Luther's wagon drew in sight of the walls of the city. It was at the noon-hour when the wagon passed through its gates. The day, the hour, the moment, had actually arrived when the famous monk was in the city. The city went wild with excitement. The citzens were sitting at their noon meal when Luther entered. Leaving their tables, they rushed into the streets, to get a glimpse of him whom the Pope sought to kill. The streets were so crowded that with difficulty Luther made his way to the hotel, in which he was to find lodging. When he stepped from his wagon to the ground, he uttered these words, "God will be my defense." And God was.

When the Emperor, Charles V, heard that Luther had arrived, he was much agitated. He said, "Luther is come, what must we do?" Luther spent the afternoon and evening at his hotel resting, what time he was not receiving visitors, who thronged the place by the scores, eager to see him. Charles V called the council to meet at four o'clock the next afternoon, and Luther was notified to that effect on the morning of that eventful day.

When the clock struck the hour of four, on the afternoon of Apr. 17, 1521, all the world waited breathlessly to see what that hour would bring forth. Martin Luther trembled, as he recognized that he was being brought before the greatest tribunal in the world. But he was brave, and he followed the marshal and the herald, who were sent to bring him into the hall. The herald went first, the marshal next, and Luther came last. But the streets were so crowded that they could not get through, and they were obliged to enter the doors of private houses, and go through back yards and gardens to the place where the council was sitting. When they reached the door of the town hall they could not get in for the people. "Make way, make way," they shouted, but no one moved. By force the soldiers cleared a way, and they pushed through the crowd into the building.

And there the son of the poor miner stood before a court as great as if not greater than, that before which a man had ever stood. This council was made up of the mighty ones of the earth— emperor, kings, barons, dukes, princes, nobles, electors, bishops, prelates, and ambassadors—in all, two hundred and four persons. As Luther stood before the dazzling throne of Charles V, all eyes were turned on him. For a time he seemed overcome with the splendor of the surroundings, and was unable to speak. For a moment terrible and awful silence reigned. An officer rose and broke the silence with these words, which he spoke first in Latin, and then in German: "Martin Luther, his sacred and invincible imperial majesty has cited you before his throne, in accordance with the advice and counsel of the states of the Holy Roman Empire, to require you to answer two questions: first, Do you acknowledge these books [on the table] to have been written by you? second, Are you prepared to retract these books, and their contents; or do you persist in the opinions you have advanced in them?" Luther owned that he had written the books. But the second question, "Will you retract them, or apologize for them?" he did not want to answer without time to think it over. The Emperor, and his counselors, agreed to give

Luther twenty-four hours, in which to decide how
he would answer that second question, "Will you
retract?" Luther went back to his hotel, and spent
most of the night in prayer. It was a terrible night
for him. It seemed at times that God had for-
saken him. He prayed again and again. Finally,
he reached the place where his heart said, "Amen,"
to God's will, and his mind was at peace. At
four o'clock in the afternoon of April 18, he was
again taken to the hall where the council was sitting. The great crowd packed the hall and court,
making the atmosphere warm and sultry. Luther
was obliged to remain outside, in the court, for two
hours or more while the council was engaged in
other matters. Here he was gazed upon by the
surging mass of friends and enemies, all anxious
to lay eyes upon the famous monk. At last, when
it had grown dark, and the candles were lighted,
Luther was again brought before the council, where
he was again asked to answer the second question
put to him the day before; namely, "Will you retract the books you have written?" Luther ad-
dressed the Emperor and the princes in the German language, using the most humble terms. He
made a rather long address, in which he apolo-
gized for some strong terms he had used against
his enemies, which terms, he granted, were unwise.

But as for retracting any of the doctrines put forth in his books, he utterly refused, unless he were first convinced that they were not in accordance with the Scripture. In case his books were proved to be unscriptural, he said that he would be the first to throw them in the fire. When Luther had finished his address in German, he was nearly worn out, but he was required to give it also in Latin, as the Emperor did not understand German. It seemed impossible for him to go on with it, but the Lord helped him, and he repeated it in Latin, with great vigor. The orator for the council was much amazed at Luther's speech, and demanded that he answer the question, "yes," or "no." To this Luther replied, "Since your most serene majesty and your high mightiness require from me a clear, simple, and precise answer I will give you one. . . . I can not, and I will not retract. . . . Here I stand; I can do no other; may God help me! Amen!" Amid great confusion, Luther was taken back to his hotel.

Chapter IX
KIDNAPPED BY FRIENDS

It was on Thursday, April 18, 1521, that Luther took his noble stand before the Emperor, and the representatives of the Pope. The whole city of Worms was in a turmoil. Everybody was excited. Many were against Luther. Many were for him. Some praised him. Others denounced him. Through it all the great reformer remained calm and unshaken. His hotel was thronged by the multitude of persons who sought to speak with him. He was busy night and day talking with friends of the Reformation, and making plans for carrying on the great work which he had begun. As to himself he knew little of what might happen to him, but in any event, his work must be carried on. His safe-conduct was about to expire, but, at the command of the Emperor, on April 26 he mounted his wagon, and started back to Wittenberg. In the wagon with him were his brother, James Luther, and two other persons. "The villain is gone. We shall do our best," said Aleander, the Pope's man, meaning, of course, that he and his helpers would do their best to see that Luther was put to death.

It has been stated before that this Aleander was

a shrewd and courteous liar, and it is not at all surprizing that Charles should have him write up the edict which was to declare the monk an outlaw. This edict was a fierce and terrible piece of writing. It declared that Luther was a beastly outlaw, and that he should be captured dead or alive, and brought before the authorities. His writings were to be burned, and his property and that of his followers was not to be respected. This edict was written by Aleander, and on the morning of May 26, just after mass in the church, it was signed by the Emperor.

Meanwhile Luther was on his way back to Wittenberg. He stopped on his way to visit his feeble old grandmother, who died soon afterward. After receiving the blessings of his grandmother, Luther resumed his journey to Wittenberg. As the wagon drew near the Castle of Altenstein, in the Thuringian Mountains, it passed through a small ravine, in following the winding road that skirted the dense woods. It was near the close of the day, and darkness was beginning to settle over the thick forest. All of a sudden a noise was heard, and there came rushing out of the dark forest, five masked men on horses. They were armed from head to foot. When James Luther saw them, he sprang from the wagon, and escaped into the woods. One of the masked men held the driver, while another one of them engaged Amsdorff, the third member of the party in the wagon. The other three masked men seized Luther bodily, set him on a horse that they led, and made their escape with him among the trees. They wandered up and down in the woods, retracing their steps now and then, in order that their trail might not be followed. Luther, unused to horseback riding, was overcome with fatigue, and was compelled to alight and rest a while near a beech-tree, where he drank from a spring that still bears his name. When Luther had rested a short while, they again mounted their horses, and continued wandering around through the forest until nearly midnight, when they came to the foot of a mountain. At the top of this hill was an old castle, which had been occupied for generations by German nobles and princes. The name of the castle was the Wartburg, and the hill on the top of which it stood was near the town of Eisenach. When the five masked men who had captured Luther came to the foot of this hill, they turned their horses' heads towards the castle at its top. They put Luther in this castle and locked him up. The people in it did not know who the newcomer was. They were told by the lord of the castle that his name was Knight

Luther Kidnapped by Friends

George, and he was known by that name during his entire stay there. He was dressed in the clothes of a knight, that is a soldier of a certain rank. He was also told to let his beard grow, which he did.

The persons who were in the wagon with Luther when he was captured drove on to Wittenberg. All along the way they spread the news of what had happened to the great Luther. He was gone. Where he was taken, and who had taken him there, they could not say. They only knew that five burly men with great swords, and mysteriously masked, silent as tombs, had carried him away. All Germany was excited. The friends of the Pope and Emperor rejoiced. The friends of Luther and the Reformation mourned. Some were sure that the Catholics had murdered him. Some reported that his dead body had been found in an old mine; and still others thought that he had escaped into Denmark, where he was sheltered by the king of that country.

I shall now tell how it was planned to capture Luther, and carry him away to the castle. It will be remembered that Frederick was Elector of Saxony, and that he was a staunch friend of Luther and his cause. Frederick knew very well of the political and religious tricks of Rome and her representatives. He was always uneasy for the welfare of the reformer. When he saw the bold stand which Luther took at Worms he knew the great danger into which the reformer was thrown. He must plan for the safety of the monk. So before Luther left Worms, Frederick sent certain persons to talk with him and learn of his plans for returning to Wittenberg. They did not let Luther know, however, of this plan to capture him lest he should object. Their plans were all laid, and when Luther and his party reached a certain point in the road they sprang upon him. Their plans were so well carried out that even Frederick did not at first, know just where Luther was in hiding, and it was well that he did not, for when Charles V asked him where Luther was he could truthfully say that he did not know.

While Luther was confined in Wartburg Castle, he often grew weary of a life so different from the exciting and active life of a few months before. From his lonely room he could look out over the dark, gloomy forest that surrounded the castle. When he looked into the mirror he scarcely knew himself, with his military clothes and long and shaggy beard and hair. The fine food which was furnished him, and the lack of exercise told on his health. Back of the castle on the hill, beside the paths, grew abundance of strawberries.

Luther was sometimes allowed to go outside the castle gate, and stroll through the woods to gather these berries. He was always attended by a guard, however. In this way Luther wandered farther and farther away from the castle in his military garb. One day he and his guard were on one of these rounds when they stopped at a convent where Luther had stayed all night a few months before, on his way to Worms. As Luther was wandering around the place one of the attendants recognized him. The guard, seeing the dangerous situation, prevailed on Luther to hasten away, and they were well on their way back to the castle before the fellow at the convent recovered from his amazement.

But the ten months which the reformer spent at the Wartburg were not a period of luxurious idleness. The little room, with its old-fashioned bed, chair, table, and wooden chest, was the scene of much labor. His pen was always busy. And a powerful pen it was. He wrote dozens and even hundreds of letters, tracts, papers, and books during his confinement. When he was first captured by the masked horsemen, many of the Catholics thought he was dead; but when the stream of writings began to pour forth from his pen they discovered, to their sorrow, that Luther was still very much alive. The greatest work that he did while in the castle was the translation of the New Testament into the German language. He based his movement upon the idea that every man should read and understand the Bible for himself. If they were to read the blessed Book, understand it, and put it into practise in their lives, they must have it translated into their own language. Luther had in his possession no dictionaries, no concordance, and no reference books. He probably had only his Greek and Latin copy, but he set to work with a will, and when he left the castle in March, 1522, the translation of the New Testament was complete. The first copies were printed at Wittenberg about seven months later, and the German people scrambled to get them, in order that they might read for themselves the blessed Word of Life. Luther's German Bible to this day is recognized as a wonderful piece of German literature.

CHAPTER X

BACK AT WITTENBERG

While Luther was quiet in his room in the Wartburg Castle, there was no quietness in his home town, Wittenberg. The city had filled up with religious cranks. From all over Germany and from many other countries of Europe these cranks came pouring into Wittenberg. These fanatics at Wittenberg were doing all sorts of silly things in the name of religion. Dr. Carlstadt lost all reason. He told the students at the University to go home and quit studying, because God was pleased to show men the truth without their studying. He put on plain workman's clothes, and was often seen going with his Bible under his arm to the most ignorant man in the whole town to have the Scriptures explained. These fanatics went into the Catholic churches, broke in pieces the images, and tore up the church furniture. They ridiculed all those who did not believe as they did. They brought great reproach on the cause of the Reformation, for the Catholics accused them of belonging to the reform party, and poor Luther was blamed for stirring up all this trouble.

All this news reached Luther's ears at the castle on the hill. When he heard it he was grieved,

He spent sleepless nights. He knew that the cause of God was suffering. But who could stop all these crazy doings at Wittenberg? The Catholics could not; the doctors and professors at Wittenberg were powerless. In fact, many of them had gone over fully to the side of the fanatics. Even Melanchthon was alarmed and knew not what to do. The wise and good elector, Frederick, was puzzled. If only Luther were there! And Luther wanted very much to be there; but if he left his hiding-place in the castle, the Pope and the Emperor would surely kill him, for he was still under the ban. The Elector would not agree for him to leave the castle. What would Luther do? He had already, in November of the previous year, stolen out of the castle, made a flying trip to Wittenberg, and returned. He wrote his friends at Wittenberg to look out for him, for he was coming again. On March 3, he stepped from behind the Wartburg walls. He said good-by to the quiet old place, and went down the hill and out into the world. In going from behind the sheltering walls of Wartburg, into the world, he knew that he might be going to his death, but he felt that it was the call of duty; so he did not falter.

Once outside the walls he began the five days' journey to Wittenberg. When he was near the city of

Jena, he was overtaken by a thunder-storm. He stopped at Black Bear hotel. He was still dressed in his soldier's garb, and of course no one even guessed that it was Luther. While he was sitting by a table reading, two young men from Switzerland, their boots and clothing drenched with mud and rain, entered the room and sat near the door. Luther soon struck up a conversation with the young men, and they told him that they were on their way to Wittenberg to attend the university there. They said that they had heard so much of Martin Luther that they were determined to see him, and they wanted to know if the stranger could tell whether or not Luther was at Wittenberg. The stranger answered that he knew Luther was not there, but that he soon would be there. The young men were greatly joyed at the prospect of seeing the famous monk. The stranger asked them how Luther was regarded in Switzerland. They replied that some almost worshiped him, and others thought he was a contemptible servant of Satan. When they had finished supper the stranger shook hands with the two young men and said, "When you get to Wittenberg, remember me to Jerome Schurff." "Whom shall we remember, sir?" replied one of the young men. "Say only that he that will soon come sends his greetings," said the stranger. A few days later when the young men, after reaching Wittenberg, called to see Dr. Schurff and Philip Melanchthon, possibly to bear them the message from the stranger, who should they see in the room but that same stranger? And here they found the "stranger" was Luther himself.

Luther was not unconscious of the danger of his position in traveling over the country when the Emperor had given orders that he was to be captured by whomsoever should meet him. However, he had felt that he simply could not stay at the Wartburg longer, when there was such need of him at Wittenberg. On his way from the castle to Wittenberg, he stopped at the small town of Borna long enough to write a letter to the Elector Frederick, his great friend and protector. Here is what he says:

"Grace and peace from God our Father, and from our Lord Jesus Christ.

"MOST SERENE ELECTOR, GRACIOUS LORD.—The events that have taken place at Wittenberg, to the great reproach of the gospel, have caused me such pain, that if I were not confident of the truth of our cause, I should have given way to despair. . . . I have sufficiently given way to your highness by passing this year in retirement. The devil knows well that I did so not through fear. I should have entered Worms had there been as many devils in the city as tiles on the housetops. Now, Duke George [Duke George was a bitter enemy of Luther. Luther had to pass through his territory to reach Wittenberg] with whom your highness frightens me, is much less to be feared than a single devil. If that which is passing at Wittenberg were taking place at Leipzig [the Duke's residence] I would immediately mount my horse to go thither, although . . . for nine whole days together it were to rain nothing but Duke Georges, and each one nine times more furious than he is. What does he think of in attacking me? Does he take Christ my Lord for a man of straw?"

Luther goes on in this letter to explain to the Elector that he is trusting in God to protect him. He appreciates what the Elector has done for him and is willing to do, but he tells him that human hands are too feeble to protect in such a time as this; so he prefers to leave all in the hands of God. In closing the letter, he says, "I have written this letter in haste, that you may not be made uneasy at hearing of my arrival. I have to do with a very different man from Duke George. He knows me well, and I know him pretty well. Given at

Borna, at the inn of the Guide this Ash Wednesday, 1522.

> "Your electoral highness'
> "Very humble servant,
> "Martin Luther."

When Luther entered the town of Wittenberg on March 6, 1522, after having spent five days on the road, it was a day of profound joy. It was like the home-coming of a father. Students, teachers, citizens, doctors, entered into the rejoicings. The following Sunday, Luther stood in the pulpit of the Wittenberg church. His coming had been noised over the city. "Luther has come! Luther has come!" was on every one's lips. The church was crowded to the doors with those who were eager to hear the hero of Worms. They breathlessly listened when he stood up to speak. He spoke, that morning, with great boldness and humility. He preached from the text, "All things are lawful unto me, but all things are not expedient." He admonished the people for the rough way in which they had been handling things, and told them that their fanatical actions were bringing reproach on the whole Reformation. He said, in his second sermon: "Compel or force any one with power I will not, for faith must be gentle and unforced. Take an example by me. I opposed indulgences and all the papists, but not with force; I only wrote, preached, and used God's Word, and nothing else. That Word, while I slept, . . . has broken the papacy more than any king or emperor ever broke it. Had I wished it, I might have brought Germany to civil war. Yes, at Worms I might have started a game which would not have been safe for the Emperor, but it would have been a fool's game. So I did nothing, but only let the Word act."

Luther preached every day for a solid week, with great fervor and power. These sermons are models of pulpit eloquence. They brought about the desired result. Common sense gained the day. Order, for the time being, was restored, fanaticism was checked, the "prophets" turned to other fields, and once more Luther was the hero of the great reformation movement.

CHAPTER XI

LUTHER IN LOVE

Luther lived in Wittenberg, in the "Black Cloister," formerly the convent there. It was not made of black stone, but of red brick. It was called the Black Cloister because of the long black robes worn by the group of monks, of which Luther had been one, who had lived there. It was very large, with long rows of cell-like rooms. It must be remembered that the Catholic Church did not allow her priests or monks to marry, and Luther and his fellow monks had lived in this convent for years without a woman there, unless perhaps a maid or two were kept to aid in housework. When Luther received the light of the Word of God along other lines, he also obtained it on the subject of ministers' marrying. He began to teach and preach that it was the privilege of a priest to marry if he so desired. This, he said, was a thousand times better than for them to remain single, and live in such shameful immorality as was practised by a great many of them. Of course, the papists railed out on him for this teaching, and called him a lustful beast. But what did Luther care for that? He had braved the storms for so many years, he was growing used to them.

When the reformers began to teach that every man had a right to marry if he so pleased, and that it was not necessary for a lot of monks to be bunched together in a convent to keep holy, the convents began to lose their population. Many monks married, and entered upon some secular occupation in order to make an honest living for their wives and families. All the monks had left Black Cloister at Wittenberg save two—Luther and one other remained. And it was a lonely life indeed. The great, gloomy building was a cheerless spot for the brave reformer.

On Jan. 29, 1499, fifteen years after Martin Luther was born, there came into the world, in a little town a few miles south of Leipzig, Germany, a baby girl. Her parents named her Catherine. When she grew older she was commonly called Katie. Her father's name was Hans von Bora. When Katie was still a baby her mother died. A few years later, Katie's father married again, and when Katie was five years old she was sent away from home to a convent school, where her father intended that she should become a nun. In this school, the little girl was shut away from the outside world. Here she spent the quiet days in prayer, teaching, reading, and doing works of charity. In this way she became quite well educated for a girl of those days, and at the age of sixteen she was consecrated a nun. Of course, it was expected that Katie would spend her whole life behind the doors of the convent. Such a life was considered by the Catholic Church as the proper life for any pious woman to lead. But when the monks, after Luther's preaching, began to leave the convents, and go out into the free and open world, then the nuns in the nunneries thought they could do likewise; and they did. Of course, to get out of the nunnery was a hard thing to do, and any one who was caught assisting a nun to escape was dealt with severely, as was also any nun who tried to escape. Then, once out of the nunnery, the nuns knew not where to go nor what to do.

On the night of April 4, 1523, three men appeared at the nunnery in the town of Grimma, where Katie, anxious to escape, was kept. These men, one of whom was a rich business man, assisted twelve of the younger nuns to escape. Katie was one of the twelve. Three of these women went to live with their relatives, but nine did not know where to go. Katie was one of the nine. They were finally brought to Wittenberg, where it was hoped that Luther would help them. He wrote a letter concerning them to his friend, George Spalatin:

"Wittenberg, April 10, 1523.

"Grace and peace. Nine fugitive nuns, a wretched crowd, have been brought to me by honest citizens of Torgau. I mean Leonard Coppe and his nephew, Wolf Tomitzsch; there is therefore no cause for suspicion. I pity them much, but most of all the others who are dying everywhere in such numbers in their cursed and impure celibacy. This sex, so very, very weak, joined by nature or rather by God to the other, perishes when cruelly separated. O tyrants! O cruel parents and kinsmen in Germany! O pope and bishops, who can curse you enough? Who can sufficiently execrate the blind fury which has taught and enforced such things? But this is not the place to do it.

"You ask what I shall do with them? First I shall inform their relatives and ask them to support the girls; if they will not I shall have the girls otherwise provided for. Some of the families have already promised me to take them; for some I shall get husbands, if I can. Their names are: Magdalene von Staupitz, Elsa von Canitz, Ave Gross, Ave von Schonfeld and her sister Margaret, Laneta von Goltz, Margaret and Catherine Zeschau and Catherine von Bora. Here are they, who serve Christ, in need of true pity. They have escaped from the cloister in miserable condition. I pray you also do the work of charity and beg some money for me from your rich courtiers, by which I can support the girls a week or two until their kinsmen or others provide for them. . . . The poor, who would willingly give, have nothing; the rich either refuse or give so reluctantly that they lose the credit of the gift with God and take up my time begging from them. Nothing is too much for the world and its way. Of my annual salary I have only ten or fifteen gulden left, besides which not a penny has been given me by my brothers or by the city. But I ask them for nothing, to emulate the boast of Paul, despoiling other churches to serve my Corinthians free. . . .

> "Farewell and pray for me,
>
> "Martin Luther."

Luther exercised himself much in finding place for these nine runaway nuns. One of them found a home in Grimma, and one, through the influence of Luther, secured a position as a teacher. Some of them returned to their relatives, and others married. Three remained in Wittenberg. Katie was one of the three: the other two were Ave Schonfeld and her sister Margaret. Luther, it seems, fell in love with Ave, but for some reason the affair did not develop into matrimony. Luther had not intended to marry. He said he was neither wood nor stone, and like any normal man had desires toward matrimony, but he saw the clouds of persecution that hung black above his head, and he expected at any time he might meet the death of the heretic. He was still under the ban of the Pope and the Emperor, and his great friend and protector, Frederick, was dead. He did not wish to marry, and leave his wife so soon a widow.

Finally, Ave Schonfeld and her sister Margaret married, and went away from Wittenberg. Only one of the nine runaway nuns was left there. Katie was the one. She was taken into the home of a rich man who had formerly been burgomaster of Wittenberg. Here she lived for two years, and became quite an expert in housekeeping, and other useful work. By her splendid traits of character, rather than by her beauty, she won the respect and admiration of all who came in contact with her. Because of her goodness she was even nicknamed "St. Catherine of Siena."

Jerome Baumgartner, a young man who lived at Nuremberg, had attended the University of Wittenberg. He had graduated from there in 1521, and had then returned to his native town. Two years later he had come back to Wittenberg, to visit his old teacher Professor Melanchthon. While in

Wittenberg he won the heart of Katie, and went back to his home town with the understanding that he was to return to Wittenberg and wed Katie. He never returned. The reason of his failure to return is not definitely known, but it was a crushing blow to the affectionate heart of the orphan girl. Luther wrote to Jerome in these words, "If you want your Katie you had best act quickly before she is given to some one else who wants her. She has not yet conquered her love for you, and I would willingly see you married to each other." But Jerome married a rich girl.

A certain Dr. Glatz sought the hand of Katie. Luther in all good faith undertook to plead the case of Dr. Glatz, and urged Katie to marry the doctor. Katie was rather frank and replied that she utterly refused to wed Dr. Glatz, but had no objection to marrying Dr. Luther. This set the reformer to thinking, as might be expected, and he married Katie the following June, as might also be expected.

CHAPTER XII

LUTHER AT HOME

Two weeks after Luther and Katie were married, they celebrated their wedding. This was June 27, 1525. It was a happy event for Luther. Many of his friends in all parts of Germany were invited, and not a few accepted. His aged father and mother were present, and greatly rejoiced. They had encouraged Luther in his marriage. Luther wrote on June 21 to a friend of the affair and said, "God has suddenly and unexpectedly caught me in the bond of holy matrimony. I intend to celebrate with a wedding breakfast on Thursday. That my parents and all good friends may be merry, my Lord Catherine and I kindly beg you to send us, at my cost and as quickly as possible, a barrel of the best Torgau beer." It seems strange to us now that as great and good a man as Martin Luther should celebrate his wedding by drinking beer. But we must bear in mind that in his early day people thought no more of drinking beer than we think now of drinking sweet cider or lemonade. Men have come to hold different standards, due to the onward march of Christianity. At the celebration the Luthers received many presents from persons of distinction. The

Elector remembered them with a gift. Martin and Katie, like most happy "newly-weds," on this occasion sat to have their picture made.

When Luther married, he created almost as big a sensation as when he had nailed the ninty-five theses to the church-door, nearly eight years before this time. The papists accused him of every vile thing imaginable, and said he had broken away from the doctrine of priestly celibacy in order that he might gratify his own passions. Most of his friends questioned the advisability of his marriage, and some of them criticized him severely. But Luther wrote to his friend Amsdorf, "I married to gratify my father, who asked me to marry and leave him descendants . . . I was not carried away by passion, for I do not love my wife that way, but esteem her as a friend." To George Spalatin he wrote, "I have made myself so cheap and despised by this marriage that I expect the angels laugh and the devils weep thereat. The world and its wise men have not yet seen how pious and sacred is marriage, but they consider it impious and devilish in me. It pleases me, however, to have my marriage condemned by those who are ignorant of God."

When Katie came to be mistress of the Black Cloister, at the touch of her hand its long halls and gloomy corridors were soon lighted up with the sunshine of domestic happiness. It changed from the gruesome abode of monkish celibates into a happy Christian home. The Luther union was a happy one. Katie loved her husband, and in return received his love. "I would not change my Katie," said he, "for France and Venice, because God has given her to me, and other women have much worse faults, and she is true to me and a good mother to my children . . . The greatest happiness is to have a wife to whom you can trust your business and who is a good mother to your children. Katie, you have a husband who loves you; many an empress is not so well off. I am rich, God has given me my nun and three children: what care I if I am in debt, Katie pays the bills."

It seems that Luther's time was so taken up with the great religious problems of the day that he gave the business of the household into the hands of his wife. She, being a woman of sound business judgment, managed things quite successfully. It is not to be supposed, however, that Luther was ruled by his wife. She seems not to have tried such a thing, and doubtless would have failed if she had. Luther says in this respect, "My wife can persuade me anything she pleases, for she has the government of the house in her hands alone. I willingly yield the direction of domestic affairs, but wish my rights to be respected. Women's rule never did any good. . . . Katie can rule the servants, but not me."

Amid the busy cares, and stormy battles of life, Luther found time to enter into the joys and sorrows of his children. Six children came to bless the Luther home. Their names were, Hans, Elizabeth, Magdalene, Martin, Paul, and Margaret. Elizabeth did not live to see her first birthday. Magdalene died when she was thirteen. The death of these two children tore the reformer's heart with grief, because his was the heart of a devoted and true father. Once, when Luther was away from home, he wrote the following letter to his little son Hans:

"Grace and peace in Christ, dear little son. I am glad to hear that you are studying and saying your prayers. Continue to do so, my son, and when I come home I will bring you a pretty present.

"I know a lovely, pleasant garden where many children are; they wear golden jackets, and gather nice apples under the trees, and pears and cherries, and purple plums and yellow plums, and sing and run and jump and are happy and have pretty little ponies with golden reins and silver saddles. I asked the man who owned the garden who they were. He said, 'They are the children who say their prayers and study and are good.' Then said I, 'Dear man, I also have a son whose name is Hans Luther; may he come into the garden and eat the sweet apples and pears and ride a fine pony and play with these children?' Then the man said, 'If he says his prayers and is good, he may come into the garden and Phil and Justy too, and when they all come they shall have whistles and drums and fifes and shall dance and shoot little crossbows.' Then he showed me a fine, large lawn in the garden for dancing, where hung real golden whistles and fine silver crossbows. But it was yet early, and the children had not finished eating, and I could not wait to see them dance. So I said to the man, 'My dear sir, I must go and write at once to my dear little Hans about all this, so that he will say his prayers and study and be good, so that he may come into the garden, and he has an Auntie Lena whom he must bring with him.' Then the man said, 'All right, go and tell him about it.' So, dear little Hans, study and say your prayers, and tell Phil and Justy to say their prayers and study too, so you may all come into the garden together. God bless you. Give Auntie Lena my love and a kiss from me.

> "Your loving father,
>
> "Martin Luther."

CHAPTER XIII

LUTHER IN DEATH

The last years of Luther's life were rather dismal, and somewhat disappointing. Although, like Wesley, a very busy man until the close of life, his greatest work was done a dozen or more years before his death. His life had been so full of battles that old age crept upon him rather prematurely. Ill health had eaten away his physical vitality, but his flaming spirit was not conquered even unto the end. In death he had his same consuming zeal for the truth, and his mighty hold upon God was unrelaxed.

His physical afflictions increased with the years, and at the age of sixty-two, in which year he died, his body was a worn and broken vessel. Not long before his death he wrote, "Old, decrepit, sluggish, weary, worn out, and now one-eyed, I write to you. Now that I am dead—as I seem to myself—I expect the rest I have deserved to be given me, but instead I am overwhelmed with writing, speaking, doing, transacting business, just as though I had never done, written, said, or accomplished anything." This at sixty-two.

The shadows of Luther's declining days were deepened by the death of his thirteen-year-old daughter, Magdalene, in 1542. He had regarded her as a most precious treasure, since she had come to bless his home soon after the death of his first daughter, Elizabeth. The lion-heart that had not been quelled by the fiercest battles that pope and emperor could wage, was melted into tears at the death of the angel child. He felt lonesome. His old friends and associates had moved away or died one by one. He frequently believed that he was going to die, and wished that he would. He felt that his work was done, but still he worked on, frequently doing as much work in a month as three ordinary men could do in that time.

But withal, he did not lose his faith in God. A few months before Luther's death his friend Melanchthon took seriously ill, and it was thought he was dying. He lost speech and became unconscious, and his eyes were set. The doctors had given him up to die. But the staunch old reformer held on to God for him. "O God," said he, "how has the devil injured this thy instrument?"

"Be of good cheer, Philip, thou shalt not die."

The sick man whispered, "Do not detain me, for God's sake do not detain me. I am on my way to my eternal rest. Let me depart; nothing better can befall me."

"No indeed, you must serve God a while yet,"

answered Luther. He brought food for the sick man, insisted that he eat it, and soon Melanchthon was on the road to recovery.

One day in January, 1546, Luther left his Katie and his home and his friends in Wittenberg, and went away. He told them good-by, and said he would soon return. He never returned alive. He was going to Mansfeld, the scene of his boyhood days, to help settle a dispute between the Counts of Mansfeld. Twice previously he had gone there on a similar errand. The Counts were brothers, but they had grown to hate each other bitterly. Luther was in too ill health to undertake the trip, but they insisted, and he took their insistence as the voice of duty—a voice to which he never turned a deaf ear. He went. He was hindered by high waters, but reached Eisleben, where a council was held, and the trouble settled. Happy at heart over the peace he helped to make, Luther made preparations to return home. He wrote a letter to Katie telling of his intention. He had written many, many letters to his dear Katie —but this was his last:

"Eisleben, February 14, 1546.

"Grace and peace in the Lord. Dear Katie, we hope to come home this week if God will. God has shown great peace to the lords, who have been reconciled in all but two or three points. It still remains to make the brothers Count Albert and Count Gebhard real brothers; this I shall undertake today and shall invite both to visit me, that they may see each other, for hitherto they have not spoken, but have embittered each other by writing. But the young lords and the young ladies, too, are happy and make parties for fools' bells and skating, and have masquerades and are all very jolly, even Count Gebhard's son. So we see that God hears prayer.

"I send you the trout given me by the Countess Albert. She is heartily happy at this union.

"Your little sons are still at Mansfeld. [Paul, Martin, and Hans had gone with their father, and were visting at Mansfeld while he transacted his business at Eisleben.] James Luther will take care of them. We eat and drink like lords here and they wait on us so well—too well, indeed, for they might make us forget you at Wittenberg. Moreover, I am no more troubled with the stone. Jonas' leg has become right bad; it is looser on the shinbone, but God will help it. [Dr. Jonas, who was with Luther at Worms, and who was with him on this trip, had hit his leg against a trunk and injured it painfully.]

"You may tell Melanchthon and Bugenhagen and Cruciger everything.

"A report has reached here that Dr. Martin Luther has left for Leipzig or Magdeburg. Such tales are invented by those silly wiseacres, your countrymen. Some say the Emperor is thirty miles from here, at Soest in Westphalia; some that the French and the Landgrave of Hesse are raising troops. Let them say and sing; we will wait on God. God bless you.

"Dr. Martin Luther."

Luther never wrote any more letters. This one was written February 14. On February 17, he took violent pains in his chest. Hot towels were applied, and he went to bed, and slept until ten o'clock, when he awoke in great pain. More hot cloths were brought, and he slept again. About two o'clock, on the morning of the 18th, he arose and went into the next room. Here he lay down on a couch. The old house—then an inn—and this room, may still be seen.

Friends hovered near him. Paul and Martin, two of his sons, had hurried from Mansfeld. Hans was not there. Poor Katie was in Wittenberg, and could not be present when her renowned husband passed beyond. She lived sadly, and alone for six years after Luther died. In 1552 she died in Torgau, and was buried there, many miles from Wittenberg, the resting-place of her husband.

Those who on that dreary morning of Feb. 18, 1546, watched around Luther's bed as the lion-hearted reformer drew near the silent river, heard him whisper this prayer: "O my heavenly Father, one God and Father of our Lord Jesus Christ, thou God of all comfort, thou God of all comfort, I thank thee that thou hast given for me thy dear son Jesus Christ, in whom I believe, whom I have preached and confessed, loved and praised, whom the wicked Pope and all the godless shame, persecute, and blaspheme. I pray thee, dear Lord Jesus Christ, let me commend my soul to thee. O heavenly Father, if I leave this body and depart I am certain that I will be with thee forever and can never, never tear myself out of thy hands. . . .

"Father, into thy hands I commend my spirit. Thou hast redeemed me, thou true God."

Dr. Jonas bowed over him and asked, "Reverend father, will you stand stedfast by Christ and the doctrine you have preached?"

"Yes," was the answer which came distinctly from the dying man's lips. This was his last word. He sank to rest in the arms of the Christ he had so fearlessly preached throughout his stormy career.

On February 19, the funeral procession started its solemn march to Wittenberg, the scene of most of his life's labors. They reached Wittenberg on February 22. Amidst the tolling of bells, the hearse containing the remains of the lion-hearted reformer, followed by his poor widowed Katie, his four orphaned children, and a great host of grief-stricken people, was driven to the castle church. The dead body of Luther was carried through the very door on which, nearly a third of a century before, he had nailed the famous theses. Pastor Bugenhagen, interrupted by his own sobs, and those of the people, preached the funeral sermon. Melanchthon, the lifelong friend and coworker of Luther, gave an address. The lid of the casket was closed, and it was placed in the vault in the church. The people returned home wailing, "Luther is dead; Luther is dead." But only the broken and battered house of clay in which he lived was dead. Luther, the real Luther, is alive forevermore.